DOUBLE
DISHING

DOUBLE DISHING

THE *DISHING* WOMEN ENTERTAIN

whitecap

Whitecap Books

Edited by Elaine Jones
Proofread by Lesley Cameron
Cover and interior design by Maxine Lea
Photographs by Magelles Photographics
Food styling by Shelley Robinson

We gratefully acknowledge Hothouse for lending us the funky plates for the food photos and Cuiscene Restaurant for the use of their space.

Printed and bound in Canada

National Library of Canada Cataloguing in Publication Data

Double dishing

Includes index.
ISBN 1-55285-353-5

1. Entertaining. 2. Cookery, Canadian—Alberta style. 3. Cookery—Alberta—Calgary. I. Chavich, Cinda.
TX731.D68 2002   642'.4   C2002-910920-5

The publisher acknowledges the support of the Canada Council for the Arts and the Cultural Services Branch of the Government of British Columbia for our publishing program. We acknowledge the financial support of the Government of Canada through the Book Publishing Industry Development Program for our publishing activities.

Important: Some of the recipes in this book call for the use of raw eggs. Pregnant women, the elderly, young children and anyone with a compromised immune system are advised against the consumption of raw eggs. You may wish to consider the use of pasteurized eggs. www.aeb.org/safety provides updated information on eggs and food safety.

CONTENTS

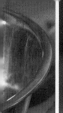

When I came to Calgary in 1982, there's no doubt it was a strictly meat and potatoes town. But, in the last 20 years, the food scene has changed dramatically —from black to white—and all for the better. The women who have joined together to write this new cookbook have definitely contributed to that change. They are all part of our local food culture. They have worked in the food business, opening specialty coffee shops and dessert places, catering, cooking, teaching and writing about good food, inspiring Calgarians to do better. By offering people different tastes or by exposing them to cooking classes and new information about fine food, all of these women have been instrumental in taking the city's cuisine to a national level.

They are not all professional chefs but, in my opinion, you don't have to be a professional as long as you have love and passion. The people in this book are individuals who stand for quality. They are creative and they promote the better foods this city has to offer.

And these are women that Calgarians know—know for their businesses, their products and their ability to inspire others.

I love to look at cookbooks. It brings ideas that motivate people to do new things at home. The first book by these talented women is beautiful with lovely photographs and a design that will lure you into its pages and this second book is a beautiful addition. But first and foremost, it's a place to start cooking. It's not always a big challenge to prepare a good meal. Start with good ingredients and instead of seeing cooking as a chore, make it a pleasure. Take the time to experiment with new foods and recipes, and enjoy gathering around the table with your family and friends.

I think it's wonderful that these talented women have put their creative food ideas into this new book. If you're not an adventurous cook, you can follow what they say to the letter. But it's not the gospel—it's a source of inspiration. We all want to inspire people to seek out quality food. Eating should not be like fueling up your car, it is a truly joyful part of life. So taste new things, try new recipes and learn from some of Calgary's best food experts. I wish them lots of luck, and hope they will continue their great efforts and the commitment they have to fine food in Calgary.

BERNARD CALLEBAUT

CINDA

PAM

DEE

KAREN

GAIL

SHELLEY

RHONDDA

JANET

JUDY

CINDA CHAVICH

Cinda has spent the past 20 years as a journalist—writing for Canadian newspapers and magazines. Specializing in food, wine and feature writing, she has travelled the world gathering stories and learning about the fascinating topic of food. But her roots are in Western Canada and her passion is in regional cuisine and telling the stories of the people who share that passion. She has written three cookbooks: the best selling *Wild West Cookbook*, *The Best Pressure Cooker Recipes*, and *High Plains: the Joy of Alberta Cuisine*.

PAM FORTIER

Pam's passion and curiosity for food began when she started to travel in her twenties. She took Professional Cooking at SAIT and then the Professional Pastry and Desserts course at Dubrulle in Vancouver. During those years, she had part-time jobs at restaurants to gain experience. In 1997, she bought Decadent Desserts in Calgary where she kept the most popular desserts but added new ones, including wedding cakes to her immense enjoyment.

dEE HOBSBAWN-SMITH

dee has been delighting Calgarian diners and readers since 1983. Her intense and dynamic food has appeared in restaurants (including her own Foodsmith), at catered events, at cooking classes, in print and on her family's table. Since selling her restaurant in 1994, she has turned her energies to writing. Her first book, *Skinny Feasts*, was published in 1997, followed by *The Quick Gourmet* in 1999. As a food writer, dee's work appears in *Canadian Living*, *Calgary* magazine, *Mountain Life*, *City Palate*, and in a weekly column in the *Calgary Herald*.

Karen Miller

Born and raised in Montreal, Karen worked as a lawyer for many years. It was not until she moved to Calgary that she had the time to pursue her interest in food. She started catering with a friend and, fuelled with positive reviews, she has balanced a full-time family and part-time catering. She loves the entertaining part of food. She is constantly preaching, either in classes she teaches or to anyone who asks, the value of food found close to the source and as unprocessed as possible.

Gail Norton

Gail's mother was a wonderful cook and family meals were always one of the highlights of the day. She has great memories of sitting around the table talking and eating tasty food. After graduating from university in 1984 with a Special Education degree, she caught the food bug and opened a bookstore with her mother that specialized in cookbooks — The Cookbook Co. In 1986, they expanded into speciality foods, catering, and Calgary's premier cooking school. Gail, for the past 10 years, has been publisher of *The City Palate* magazine.

Shelley Robinson

Shelley's passion for food and hospitality began very young. She had wonderful grandparents who believed and lived gathering and cooking foods from the Okanagan Valley. Her love of food, coupled with her strong artistic desire, led her to attend Dubrulle cooking school in Vancouver and apprentice with some of Canada's best-known chefs. Shelley's modern, eclectic cuisine has been the delight of several Calgary restaurants, including her own, countless catering clients, cooking classes and appreciative family and friends. Her current interests include the pursuit of food styling and cookbook art direction, an organic produce business distributing certified products from B.C. and Alberta and a Corporate Executive Chef position with Aramark Canada.

Rhondda Siebens

Rhondda grew up with a grandmother who instilled in her a love for home-made food and was raised by a mother who, though she loved good food, was a staunch supporter of the fast food industry. Rhondda studied International Relations and Arms Control but felt she could make a greater contribution to world peace by satisfying people's caffeine cravings. After working at Twin Falls Chalet in Yoho National Park she became enamoured with the food and beverage industry and for almost 10 years now she has been applying her diplomacy skills as proprietor of the funky Caffè Beano coffee house.

Janet Webb

Janet had a love of cooking from an early age. In the 1970s, she worked at restaurants while attending college. Later, she was the wine sommelier at the Westin Hotel in Calgary and then she maintained the wine cellar at La Caille Restaurant. In the 1980s she opened one of Alberta's first privately owned wine boutiques. After studying with Madeline Kamman at the Beringer Cooking School in California, she returned to Calgary to share her knowledge of pairing food and wine.

Judy Wood

Born in Montreal, Judy received her "Grand Diplome" from the famed L'Ecole de Cuisine La Varenne in Paris before working at the Four Seasons Hotel in Calgary, as a pastry chef at the David Wood Food Shop in Toronto, and then as the Head Chef at Buchanan's in Calgary. In 1990, she joined Sunterra Food group as Executive Chef and creative director of "all things food." In 1998, she became the Founder and Executive Chef of Savoury Café & Catering. She received the Woman of Vision award in Calgary in 1999 and can currently be seen as the Saturday chef on the *Global News* morning edition.

Potato Sorrel Soup
Green Chili Chicken Enchiladas
Grilled Sea Bass on a Bed of Pears
Chicken Breast Brochettes with Moroccan
Chermoula and Chili Glazed Baby Back Ribs
with Cinnamon Couscous and Warmed
Lentils Dressed with Walnut Oil Vinaigrette
Mango and Duck Salad with
Tangerine Dressing
Salmon with Roasted Artichoke
Tomato and Olive Sauce
Raisin Squares with Caramel
Crème Fraîche Ice Cream

MENU PLANS

Mediterranean Mezes

Tuna Tapenade on Toast, page 54

Israeli Couscous with Lamb, Vegetables
& Chickpeas, page 152

Fig & Prosciutto Pizza, page 28

Shrimp in Flak Jackets of Prosciutto
& Roasted Garlic, page 44

Roasted Tomato-Stuffed Peppers,
page 180

Chocolate & Cherry Mosaic Biscotti,
page 197

Whether you call them tapas or mezes, pinchos or mezethes, the Mediterranean way of sharing small plates of food and wine around the table is a delightful way to dine. These savoury snacks can be served on tiny plates, speared on skewers or served hot, cold or at room temperature. The great thing about this kind of dining is that it's flexible. Add or subtract dishes or augment with take-out treats. Include a selection of French, Spanish and Italian wine and you can feast with very little fuss.

Put out some small plates, a pile of napkins and some cutlery. Make sure you have a bottle of delicious olive oil on the table for dipping and a selection of cheeses. Set out a few bowls of nuts and olives, then pass the tuna tapenade and toasts. A room-temperature dish that can be prepared ahead, like the couscous, is a great first course. Have a glass of wine and then grill the shrimp. Bring out the next plate—the pizza or the stuffed peppers—when the time seems right. End your meal with espresso, biscotti and slices of orange drizzled with honey and sprinkled with cinnamon.

Like a tapas bar in Spain or a rustic outdoor taverna in Greece, it's all about taking the time and noshing with friends.

Cinda Chavich

BRUNCH FOR THE BUNCH

Fig & Prosciutto Pizza, page 28

Prairie Fruit Salad (or Depression Fruit Salad), page 208

Grilled Caesar Salad with Minted Dressing & Parmesan Chips, page 86

Brie in Silk Pyjamas with Brioche Crostini, page 228

Roasted Garlic & Cheese Soufflé, page 174

Caramel Pecan Banana Pumpkin Muffins, page 194

Hazelnut & White Chocolate Blondies with Whiskey Ice Cream, page 216

Well, there is luscious brunch for the bunch, featuring laid-back conversation, a sunny patio, champagne bubbles tickling your nose, and peace. And then there's brunch as live theatre, starring you, stumbling in a caffeine-deprived haze into your kitchen to cobble together some last-minute dishes.

Plan ahead—and cook ahead, too—so you can drink your morning latte at leisure and still have time to shower, walk the dog, clear the couch of the kids' stuff, and heat the oven before your mother-in-law arrives. Much of this menu can be made ahead, including the pizza—just add the green onions and prosciutto when you reheat the rounds.

DEE HOBSBAWN-SMITH

The Rites of Spring

Fresh-Shucked Oysters with a Demi-Sec
Vouvray Vinaigrette Drizzle, page 40

Spinach, Lemon & Thyme Soup, page 84

Herb-Crusted Lamb Chops with Olive
Aïoli, page 118

My Favourite Asparagus Salad, page 92

Tarte au Fromage Blanc (Curd Cheese
Tart), page 223

My favourite season, what with bright green asparagus hitting the markets, my sorrel, spinach and herbs poking their heads through the soil in my garden, and the butcher happily boasting the return of spring lamb. This is a menu that highlights all that's good about spring!

All you need to round out the menu is the best loaf of crusty sourdough bread you can find.

Janet Webb

SUMMERTIME AND THE EATING IS EASY

Thai Prawns with Toasted Sesame Seeds,
page 45

Grilled Scallops with Lemon & Roasted
Pepper Relish, page 46

Haricot Vert Salad with Figs & Walnut
Vinaigrette, page 88

Grilled Caesar Salad with Minted Dressing
& Parmesan Chips, page 86

Wrapped Chicken with Sage &
Prosciutto, page 127

Braised Fennel with Rosemary Honey
& Balsamic Vinegar, page 179

Hazelnut & White Chocolate Blondies
with Whiskey Ice Cream, page 216

Not all barbecues and picnics have to be about hot dogs and
hamburgers. Not that there's anything wrong with that, but sometimes it's fun to step outside the box.

This is best served on an isolated, sandy beach with lots of friends
and/or family and some carefully chosen beverages. No gas barbecue here. Just dig down in the sand, pile up your charcoal and
some applewood chips, lay down your oversized grill and begin
the adventure. Of course, not many of us can actually do this. It's
nice to dream though, isn't it? Fire up your backyard barbecue or
campfire and get started.

JUDY WOOD

A FRENCH COUNTRY DINNER

Salted Foie Gras, page 38

Walnut Salad, page 93

Duck Legs with Cabbage & Tomatoes,
page 150

Bartlett Pears Poached in Saffron Star
Anise & Black Peppercorn Sauternes, page 212

This is a fall or winter menu, rich and comforting.

Start off with some pastis to set the French tone, maybe with
some fennel-scented olives to stimulate the palate. Sit down to
the foie gras, served with toasted baguette or brioche slices, and
savour its wonderful, silky richness. After the foie gras, the walnut
salad is clean-tasting, with its fresh greens and the season's new
crop of walnuts. The duck, which has been perfuming the house
since the guests arrived, is luscious and rich, served on a mound
of steaming mashed potatoes or a mixture of mashed parsnips
and celery root. When your guests are ready for dessert, the clear
taste of the pears in Sauternes, with the haunting note of star
anise and a slight bite of black pepper, provide just the right finishing note.

PAM FORTIER

A REAL COCKTAIL PARTY

Set out: Hot-Smoked Trout with Caper
Aïoli, page 52

Beef Roulades with Cambozola Butter,
page 58

Cedar-Planked Brie with Roasted Garlic,
page 37

Hot & Passed: Rosemary Potato Pizza,
page 30

Rack of Lamb with Balsamic Demi, page 112

Grilled Scallops with Lemon & Roasted
Pepper Relish, page 46

Cold & Passed: Smashed Soybean &
Garlic Crostini with Shaved Parmesan, page 36

Salted Foie Gras, page 38

Tuna Tapenade on Toast, page 54

By cocktail party, I mean real drinks, cocktails with fancy glasses
and all, not just beer and wine. I mean real attention to the
invites, not just all your "must pay backs."

A cocktail party can be 8 people or 100 people, but it should
always be lively. Sophisticated but fun, something to be talked
about for weeks (and not because Mrs. Jones shimmied on the coffee table). The food is important but not front and centre, and
because of that, it must be appealing, full of flavour and easy to eat
while holding your drink. Cocktail parties should not start at eight
nor should they go on to midnight. Start at five and let your guests
know it's time to leave by eight. It should not be a slumber party.

When calculating quantities, think four bites per person per hour
and that they will be there for two hours. Have lots of cocktail
napkins for both drinks and food.

It would be wonderful if we all had a kitchen staff to cook and
serve the food but, alas, we do not. If the party is big enough,
get someone to pass the food and keep the bar clean. Otherwise,
be organized and keep it simpler. Set food out by the platterful
and pick a tray up once in a while to make your way into a group.

Finally, you are strictly instructed to enjoy yourself immensely.
When the music starts skipping and the last guest leaves, kick
your shoes off and revel in your success.

KAREN MILLER

TASTING MENU
(MENU DE DÉGUSTATION)

Amuses Bouches: Tuna Tapenade on
Toast, page 54

Fresh-Shucked Oysters with a Demi-Sec
Vouvray Vinaigrette Drizzle, page 40

Mini Blini Cornets Stuffed with Cold-Smoked
Salmon Mousse & Crystallized Lemon, page 50

Roasted Garlic & Cheese Soufflé, page 174

Watercress, Kumquat & Pine Nut Salad
with Champagne Vinaigrette, page 90

Shiitake Mushrooms & Sherry Soup, page 74

Salted Foie Gras (page 38) on Haricot Vert
Salad with Figs & Walnut Vinaigrette, page 88

Rosemary & Pear Cider Sorbet with
Cider-Poached Pear, page 213

Pappardelle with Truffles & Cream, page 160

Sansho-Peppered Tuna with Mock-Guac,
page 125

Grilled Lamb Chops with Molasses Glaze
& Tomato Prosciutto Sauce, page 116

A Trio of Ice Creams: Caramel Roasted Pears
with Pernod, page 214; Hazelnut & White
Chocolate Blondies with Whiskey, page 216;
Rosewater & Sage Ice Cream, page 218

Mignardises: Chocolate & Cherry Mosaic
Biscotti, page 197

Brown Sugar Pecan Cookies, page 196

My Mother's Shortbread Cookies, page 193

The tasting menu, or *menu de dégustation*, is my favourite way to
entertain as it allows me to really "strut" my skills and try out new
items and plating. This will not be for every cook, nor will it suit
all diners, but let me give you a few of the reasons why you may
or may not choose to enter the world of culinary hedonism.

It is a long event, usually taking up to 3 hours to experience,
depending on the number of courses served. This provides a

wonderful platform for conversation among guests, truly a luxury in our fast-paced lives.

The menu and the planning thereof is no small task; preparation and shopping in most cases will have to begin days ahead. You will need to decide what china, glassware and cutlery you will use with each menu item; if your supply does not accommodate the number of guests and courses planned, you may need to rent or borrow the balance. As the menu serves the same item to each guest, it is imperative that you find out food allergies and diet restrictions in advance.

If you want to actually enjoy the event as well, do yourself a huge favour and hire at least one person to help you clear and serve.

If you are not discouraged yet, good! You will be madly appreciated by your guests; a menu tasting is a special event and will be remembered for years to come.

The menu here is designed using a traditional triangle course-building method. It begins with smaller, more delicate flavours and builds up to finish the meal on a heavy note. Keep in mind that each course should be at most 2 or 3 mouthfuls; your guests should be left hanging on the last bite, wanting more. The first course—*amuses bouches*—is intended to invigorate, or open up, the palate. The number of courses that come next can vary and the menu ends with the *mignardises*, exquisite small treats to top off an already extravagant event.

SHELLEY ROBINSON

Vegetarian Dinner Party

Haricot Vert Salad with Figs & Walnut
Vinaigrette, page 88

Miso-Braised Mushrooms on a Polenta
Bed, page 156

My Favourite Asparagus Salad (omit the
Parmesan), page 92

Smashed Soybean & Garlic Crostini with
Shaved Parmesan (omit the Parmesan), page 36

Rosemary & Pear Cider Sorbet with
Cider-Poached Pear, page 213

No need to get in a panic when your dinner guests state that
they're vegetarians, but be aware of the type of vegetarians that
they are. Don't ever assume, as I have in the past, that you can
just substitute a nice piece of fish for the steaks that you were
going to throw on the barbecue. Lacto-ovo vegetarian, pisco-
lacto-ovo vegetarian or vegan—frankly, it makes sense to just
cover all the bases and go for the completely vegan meal—no
animal products at all. (For this menu, omit the Parmesan from
the asparagus salad and crostini recipes.) You might be surprised
how much you like it!

Rhondda Siebens

KILLER POTLUCK

Shrimp with a Coconut Lemon Grass
Glaze, page 42

Fig & Prosciutto Pizza, page 28

Salad Towers of Slow-Roasted Tomatoes,
Prosciutto, Parmesan & Greens, page 91

Pork Tenderloin with Rhubarb Chutney,
page 130

Braised Fennel with Rosemary Honey
& Balsamic Vinegar, page 179

My Favourite Asparagus Salad, page 92

"Creamsicle" Tart, page 224

I love having people over and there's no better way than over good food and drink. It's a great way to keep in touch with friends and an excuse to invite new people as well. But even thinking about entertaining in the midst of all our insane schedules seems to be half the battle—and finding a group of people that are compatible and available on a specific date is no small feat. My strategy is to have what I have coined "killer potluck"; I get a group together and ask each person to bring a course. It is always fun and lively, bringing everyone into the conversation of the meal that's being prepared. Guests who don't know each other have the food as a conversation piece (hey, great textural elements; where on earth did you find dried strawberries?; you made the phyllo dough yourself . . . what, are you nuts?).

This allows me to entertain friends more often, the contributing chefs can share the spotlight, and I get to experience dishes I would not normally make. Of course, this means only having friends who are good cooks or at least up for the game.

One frequent customer and accomplished but fearful cook once complained that I never had him and his wife over for dinner. I shot back, "Okay, next Saturday a bunch of us are getting together and everyone is bringing a dish." His eyes got a bit wider as he imagined snobby food critics sitting around the table dismantling his creation. And having a perverse sense of humour, I thought I would add to the pressure and mentioned that the dish had to be properly garnished and sauced. His eyes really popped then, but all was well, because people who are being well-fed are an enthusiastic audience, and the object of any get-together is the company. The food is merely gilding an already shiny lily.

GAIL NORTON

BEGINNINGS

PASSED HORS D'OEUVRES AND PLATED APPETIZERS

Fig & Prosciutto Pizza

I love big flavour combinations and this pizza has everything. It is messy, so I like to make it in individual rounds, but by all means make it in more traditional sizes and enjoy all its richness. You can make your own fig jam by combining equal portions of fresh figs and sugar, bringing to a boil and simmering until soft and gooey. As a shortcut, buy a good-quality jam (such as LuLu's) in a specialty food store or at your local farmers' market.

RECOMMENDED WINE: soft, fruity zinfandel from California or primitivo from Italy

KAREN MILLER

MAKES ABOUT 40 MINIATURE PIZZA ROUNDS

1 recipe	Pizza Dough	1 recipe
2 tsp.	olive oil	10 mL
1/2 tsp.	minced garlic	2.5 mL
	sea salt and freshly ground black pepper to taste	
1 tsp.	chopped fresh rosemary	5 mL
1/4 cup	fig jam	60 mL
4 oz.	Gorgonzola, crumbled	113 g
4 oz.	prosciutto	113 g
	cornmeal, for sprinkling	
1	green onion, slivered, for garnish	1

Preheat the oven to 450°F (230°C). Roll out the pizza dough until quite thin. Using a 3-inch (7.5-cm) pastry cutter, cut it into individual rounds. Brush the top surface of each round with olive oil and sprinkle the garlic over top. Salt and pepper the rounds and add the chopped rosemary. Dot each round with a little jam and a small piece of cheese, and top with a piece of prosciutto. Bake on a pizza pan sprinkled with cornmeal until the pizza is browned, about 12 to 13 minutes. Garnish with green onion slivers when it comes out of the oven.

Pizza Dough

1 Tbsp.	active dry yeast	15 mL
1 tsp.	honey	5 mL
$\frac{1}{4}$ cup	warm water	60 mL
3 cups	bread flour	720 mL
1 tsp.	salt	5 mL
2 Tbsp.	olive oil	30 mL
$\frac{3}{4}$ cup	water	180 mL

Dissolve the yeast and honey in the $\frac{1}{4}$ cup (60 mL) warm water. In an electric mixer with a dough hook combine $1\frac{1}{2}$ cups (360 mL) of the flour and the salt. Add the olive oil and then the yeast mixture. Stir in the $\frac{3}{4}$ cup (180 mL) water and gradually add the rest of the flour. Knead until the dough is smooth and firm and pulls away from the side of the bowl. Place in an oiled bowl, cover with plastic wrap and let rise until doubled, about 30 minutes. Divide into 3 balls. Let rest for about 10 to 15 minutes under a damp tea towel. On a lightly floured surface, roll out the balls from the middle into 8-inch (20-cm) rounds.

ROSEMARY POTATO PIZZA

Okay, I'll admit that the idea of potato pizza is not something that most people will immediately be excited about. But if you like potatoes, rosemary, olive oil and provolone cheese, then I think you will find this as delicious as I do!

RECOMMENDED WINE:
Italian Chianti, dolcetto or barbera

PAM FORTIER

SERVES 6 TO 8 AS AN APPETIZER

For the pizza dough:

2 cups	warm water	480 mL
	pinch sugar	
4 tsp.	active dry yeast	20 mL
5–6 cups	all-purpose flour	1.2–1.5 L
4 Tbsp.	olive oil	60 mL
1 tsp.	salt	5 mL

If using regular yeast, place the water, sugar, yeast and $1/2$ cup (120 mL) of the flour in a large bowl. Stir to combine and let stand until foamy, about 15 minutes. Whisk in the olive oil and salt. (If using instant yeast, place the water, sugar, yeast, olive oil, salt and $1/2$ cup/120 mL of the flour in a large bowl. Whisk for approximately 1 minute, then proceed as follows.) Add the remaining flour by the half cup (120 mL), whisking it in after each addition. Switch to a wooden spoon when the whisk starts to become clogged.

When the dough loses some of its stickiness, turn it out onto a flour-dusted counter. Knead in the remaining flour, a couple of tablespoons (30 mL) at a time, until the dough is soft, springy and no longer sticky. This should take 3 to 5 minutes. Place in a bowl that has been greased with olive oil. Cover with plastic wrap, then a clean kitchen towel. Allow to rise at room temperature until doubled in size, approximately $1 1/2$ hours.

Punch down to deflate. Shape into a large oval on an oiled cookie sheet.

ROSEMARY FOR
REMEMBRANCE

Once you have the scent
of rosemary in your life,
it's hard to forget it.
Rosemary is reminiscent
of pine and eucalyptus, its
sharply pungent aroma
tinged with a finish of
camphor. In the world of
natural healing, rosemary is
credited with being a tonic
for the memory,
stimulating mental clarity.
In the kitchen, a little fresh
rosemary goes a very long
way, adding a warm and
woody note to red meat,
especially lamb and game.

DEE HOBSBAWN-SMITH

For the rosemary potato topping:

3	potatoes, preferably russet, peeled and coarsely grated	3
2 Tbsp.	finely chopped fresh rosemary	30 mL
3 cups	grated provolone cheese	720 mL
1/2 cup	extra virgin olive oil	120 mL
	pinch chili flakes	
	salt and freshly ground black pepper to taste	

Preheat the oven to 400°F (200°C). Place the potatoes in a fine strainer and rinse under cold water until the water runs clear. Let drain while chopping the rosemary and grating the cheese. Place the potatoes in a clean kitchen towel and squeeze the ends in opposite directions to remove as much water as possible. Heat the olive oil in a frying pan over medium heat. Add the potatoes, rosemary, chili flakes, salt and pepper. Sauté for approximately 10 minutes. Taste again and adjust the seasonings if needed.

Sprinkle the grated cheese evenly over the unbaked pizza shell. Scatter the potatoes evenly over the cheese. Bake for approximately 15 to 20 minutes, or until the crust is golden.

LEEK & BRIE FLATBREAD

Patience is the key here. Take the time to let the leeks cook properly and they will sweeten up to perfection. This is not the time to count grams of fat.

RECOMMENDED WINE: if this is used as a munchy pre-dinner, then an Alsatian Crement d'Alsace or riesling would go great

JUDY WOOD

MAKES 48 CIRCLES

1 Tbsp.	butter	15 mL
1	leek, thinly sliced	1
1/2 cup	white wine	120 mL
1/2 cup	cream	120 mL
	salt and freshly ground black pepper to taste	
2 tsp.	active dry yeast	10 mL
2 cups	all-purpose flour	480 mL
1 cup	water	240 mL
2 tsp.	oil	10 mL
1 tsp.	salt	5 mL
8 oz.	Brie	225 g

Melt the butter in a pan over medium-high heat. Add the leek and cook until all the liquid has evaporated, about 5 minutes. Add the white wine and continue to cook until the wine is almost all gone. Repeat with the cream. Season with salt and pepper.

Place the yeast and flour in a mixer with a dough hook and mix well. Add the water, oil and salt. Mix for about 5 minutes.

Place the dough in a bowl and let rise for 15 to 20 minutes.

Preheat the oven to 425°F (220°C). Roll the dough out on a floured work surface to a thickness of about 1/8 inch (.3 cm). Cut into 1.5-inch (3.75-cm) circles and bake for 1 minute. Roll them flat. Top each circle with the leek mixture and then a slice of Brie. Bake for 3 to 5 minutes and serve immediately.

Grilled Scallops with Lemon & Roasted Pepper Relish (p. 46)

Sesame-Crusted Salmon Satés with Orange Ginger (p. 47), Nori Rolls
with Grilled Vegetables & Chévre (p. 64) and Provençal Tarts (p. 56)

Mini Blini Cornets Stuffed with Cold-Smoked Salmon Mousse &
Crystallized Lemon (p. 50)

Pumpkin Soup with Maple Syrup Caramelized Croutons (p. 78)

Canadian Ploughman

RECOMMENDED WINE:
Canadian pinot gris, pinot noir or baco noir

A ploughman's lunch is a standard in British pubs. Several slices of cheese and bread, pickles and maybe a bit of meat—nothing fancy, just what a farmer might have wrapped up to take out to the field with him. At my restaurant, Foodsmith, I Canadianized the idea and made it fit our constantly evolving menu. So the "Canadian Ploughman" became a savoury cheesecake, different every week, served with baguette, pickled red onions and gherkins. Slice it and plate tiny wedges as a first course, or present it whole, with cheese knives. Vary the flavour, as you would any cheesecake, by altering the flavouring ingredients. Just don't forget the pickles!

SERVES 15 TO 25   DEE HOBSBAWN-SMITH

2.2 lbs.	Canadian cream cheese	1 kg
2 cups	sour cream	480 mL
4	eggs	4
½ lb.	crumbled blue, Asiago or Parmesan cheese	225 g
4 Tbsp.	minced fresh parsley	60 mL
2 Tbsp.	minced mixed fresh herbs (dill, thyme, rosemary, oregano, marjoram)	30 mL
1	12-oz. (340-mL) can artichoke hearts, quartered	1
½ cup	roasted red bell pepper strips (see page 46)	120 mL
2 Tbsp.	butter, softened	30 mL
¼ cup	dried fine bread crumbs	60 mL

Preheat the oven to 300°F (150°C).

Cream the cream cheese and sour cream in a mixer or food processor. Add the eggs and blend well. Stir in the crumbled cheese, parsley and mixed herbs, artichoke hearts and red pepper strips, mixing gently to blend.

Butter the inside and bottom of a 10-inch (25-cm) springform pan. Sprinkle the pan with the bread crumbs, discarding any that do not stick.

Gently pour the cream cheese mixture into the pan. Bake for about 1 hour, or until just set. Do not overbake. Cool, then chill overnight before serving.

FLAX & OAT FLAT BREAD WITH BASIL, CHEDDAR & OLIVE OIL

A good homemade bread of any shape is always a welcome sight, and the scent of bread baking will put any guest into a receptive mood. Chewy texture and good mouth feel in a slightly rustic style make for a wonderful light lunch or brunch dish, a hearty aside to any soup or stew, and the perfect savoury for whenever you need a nosh. (Late-night movies are a perfect match for leftovers!) Extra dough makes lovely boules, or rounds.

DEE HOBSBAWN-SMITH   MAKES 4 8-INCH (20-CM) ROUNDS

2 Tbsp.	yeast	30 mL
2 Tbsp.	sugar	30 mL
1/4 cup	warm-to-hot water or milk	60 mL
2 1/2 cups	all-purpose flour	600 mL
1 1/4 cups	whole wheat flour	300 mL
1 1/2 cups	quick-cooking rolled oats	360 mL
1 Tbsp.	kosher salt	15 mL
2 Tbsp.	flax seed	30 mL
2–4 Tbsp.	olive oil	30–60 mL
2 cups	warm-to-hot water (or milk)	480 mL
6 Tbsp.	extra virgin olive oil	90 mL
1 cup	diced and seeded tomatoes	240 mL
4 Tbsp.	finely minced fresh basil	60 mL
4	cloves garlic, sliced into shards	4
2 Tbsp.	chopped fresh parsley	30 mL
1 tsp.	minced fresh rosemary	5 mL
2 Tbsp.	minced fresh thyme	30 mL
3	green onions, minced	3
1 cup	grated sharp Cheddar cheese	240 mL
	kosher salt and freshly ground black pepper to taste	

In a mixer, combine the yeast, sugar and 1/4 cup (60 mL) warm water or milk. Let this mixture stand for about 5 minutes, until it is puffy. Add the flours, oats, salt, flax seed, olive oil and 2 cups (480 mL) water or milk. Mix with the dough hook until it forms a smooth ball, about 5 minutes, adding flour as needed.

Turn the dough out onto the counter and knead by hand for 3 to 5 minutes, until smooth and soft. Oil the bowl with 1–2 Tbsp. (15–30 mL) of the extra virgin olive oil, turn the dough into the bowl, cover with plastic wrap and put in a warm place to rise. Rising time depends on the temperature, but expect 40 to 60 minutes in a warm room.

When the dough has doubled in bulk, punch it down and divide it into 4 equal pieces. Knead each piece briefly, for 1 to 2 minutes, and shape into 4 flat rounds about 8 inches (20 cm) in diameter, using the flat of your hand to shape and flatten the surface. Leave a $\frac{1}{2}$-inch (1.2-cm) raised lip around each circle of dough. Let the loaves rise again until doubled in bulk, about 15 to 30 minutes, depending on the ambient temperature.

Preheat the oven to 375°F (190°C). Place the rounds on parchment-lined baking sheets. Evenly divide the tomatoes, basil, garlic, parsley, rosemary, thyme, onions and Cheddar cheese among the 4 rounds, arranging the toppings in a way that pleases your eye. Drizzle each round with the remaining 4–5 Tbsp. (60–75 mL) extra virgin olive oil, then sprinkle each with salt and pepper.

Bake the flatbreads until nicely brown and crusty, about 10 minutes. Cut each round into 8 wedges with a pizza wheel and serve with napkins. Serve hot or at room temperature.

Smashed SOYBEAN & GARLIC
CROSTINI WITH SHAVED Parmesan

These little morsels are so inviting, strutting their bright green colour! People eat them without even knowing what they are, demand the recipe and show complete surprise when they find out what the ingredients are. Soybeans are available in the pod or shelled in the frozen vegetable section at Asian markets. Save yourself the hassle and buy them already shelled.

RECOMMENDED WINE:
Aperitif—bubbly of some sort or crisp Italian white

JANET WEBB

MAKES ABOUT 2 DOZEN

2 lbs.	frozen shelled soybeans, about 1³⁄₄ cups (420 mL)	900 g
2 Tbsp.	olive oil	30 mL
2–3	cloves garlic, finely minced	2–3
2 tsp.	fresh lemon juice	10 mL
	kosher salt and freshly ground black pepper to taste	
1	loaf baguette	1
¹⁄₄ cup	olive oil	60 mL
24	curls Parmesan cheese, shaved with a vegetable peeler	24

Bring a medium pot of water to a boil and add the soybeans. Boil for 5 to 7 minutes, then drain and rinse under cold water. Place the soybeans, the 2 Tbsp. (30 mL) olive oil, garlic and lemon juice in the bowl of a food processor and pulse to create a chunky paste. Season with salt and pepper.

Preheat the broiler and adjust the rack to the upper third area. Slice the baguette on the diagonal in ¹⁄₄- to ¹⁄₃-inch-thick (.6- to .85-cm) slices. Using a pastry brush, paint both sides of each slice with the ¹⁄₄ cup (60 mL) olive oil. Arrange the slices on baking sheets, and broil one sheet at a time for approximately 1 to 2 minutes, until golden (broiling time will vary with each oven). Turn the slices over and return to the broiler for another 1 to 2 minutes. Allow the slices to cool. (The crostini may be made up to 2 days in advance and kept in an airtight container. For a smokier flavour, make the crostini on the grill.)

To serve, spread a teaspoon (5 mL) or so of the soybean mixture on each crostini. Place 1 Parmesan curl on each crostini. Add more freshly ground black pepper to taste, if desired. Serve immediately.

Cedar-Planked Brie with Roasted Garlic

RECOMMENDED WINE: crisp, dry riesling from Germany or a simple, fruity red, like a gamay or pinot noir

ROASTING GARLIC

I have two methods for roasting garlic. For the oven method, slice the top off the garlic bulb, exposing the individual cloves. Drizzle it with oil and place it in a 350°F (175°C) oven until it softens, about 1 hour. Squeeze the cloves out of the husks. The stovetop method is my personal preference. For this, break the bulb into individual cloves and peel—easily done by whacking them with the flat side of a wide chef's knife first. Place the peeled cloves in a small pan and cover with olive oil. Roast over low-medium heat on the stovetop until the cloves are light golden and soft. Strain the beautifully infused garlic olive oil and set it aside for another use. The cloves can be left whole or puréed, depending on the dish.

SHELLEY ROBINSON

A great appetizer, snack or light lunch with a salad. Who can resist warm cheese and sweet garlic? You can purchase cedar planks at home improvement stores that sell lumber. For this recipe you need a 5- x 5-inch (12.5- x 12.5-cm) untreated plank. I bought fence-post tops that are the perfect size and are thick enough to endure several uses on the barbecue. Wash the cedar plank thoroughly, but do not use the dishwasher—I have found the heat and moisture will warp the plank.

SERVES 2 TO 4   SHELLEY ROBINSON

½ cup	roasted and roughly chopped garlic	120 mL
½ cup	chutney or chunky fruit jam (fig or mango is great)	120 mL
½-lb.	round of Brie or Camembert	225-g
	crackers or slices of fresh bread	

Preheat the barbecue to medium-high. Mix the roasted garlic and chutney or jam together and top the Brie or Camembert with it. Place the cheese on the plank and put the plank directly on the grill. Cover the cheese with a lid that does not squash the cheese or the topping (an aluminum pie plate or roasting pan lid will do). The plank will begin to smoke and the cheese will soften in about 5 to 8 minutes.

Remove from the grill and place the plank on a serving tray garnished with crackers or fresh bread slices. Serve immediately while the plank is still smoking for a dramatic effect!

Salted Foie Gras

In this recipe, inspired by a dish in Susan Loomis's *French Farmhouse Cookbook*, the salt "cooks" the foie gras so no heating is required. The curing process makes for a smooth, densely packed consistency. With some other foie gras preparations, such as grilling, much of the foie gras is lost in the cooking process. This preparation has the advantage of not losing any volume. Salted foie gras is great shaved as a garnish on vegetable or salad dishes. Or broil a thin slice on a piece of baguette until it is just starting to melt—simple and divine.

RECOMMENDED WINE: California viognier, Alsatian pinot gris or a dry malvasia

GAIL NORTON

SERVES 10 TO 20

1	medium (about 2 lbs./1 kg) foie gras	1
4–6 cups	milk	1–1.5 L
6 cups	kosher salt	1.5 L
2 Tbsp.	coarsely ground black pepper	30 mL

Remove the foie gras from the fridge 2 hours before you plan to work with it, so it has time to come to room temperature. Remove the nerves that run through the middle of the lobes of foie gras. Don't be intimidated by this process; the nerves are very easily distinguished from the foie gras "flesh" and are easily removed (and it is over quickly). Pull the lobes apart with your hands, then firmly grip one end of the nerves and pull. Press the foie gras back together into the lobe shape.

Heat the milk over low heat until it's lukewarm. (The milk must not be so hot that it melts the foie gras. Test the milk on the inside of your wrist for temperature; if your wrist can't feel the drop of milk, the temperature is perfect.) Place the foie gras in a large bowl and cover it with the warmed milk. Let it sit in the milk, turning it if necessary so that it is evenly covered, until it has softened, about 5 minutes.

Remove the foie gras from the milk and wrap it firmly in a single layer of tightly-woven cheesecloth, tying the ends together so the foie gras is tightly bound.

Sprinkle a $\frac{1}{2}$-inch (1.2-cm) layer of salt on the bottom of a shallow pan. Add the foie gras, still wrapped in cheesecloth. Completely and generously cover the foie gras with the salt, making sure the salt is solidly packed around the lobe with no gaps. Cover the container with foil and refrigerate for 7 hours.

Remove the foie gras from the salt, brushing it lightly to remove any salt clinging to it. Unwrap and discard the cheesecloth. Gently press the cured lobe of foie gras into a long log-shape about 3 inches (7.5 cm) in diameter, then press the pepper all over the outside of the foie gras, so it is black on the surface. You may either serve the foie gras immediately or return it to the fridge for an hour or so before slicing and serving.

To serve, thinly slice the foie gras and arrange it on a chilled serving plate. It can also be shaved onto a salad (such as the Haricot Vert Salad with Figs on page 88) as a garnish.

FRESH-SHUCKED OYSTERS WITH A DEMI-SEC VOUVRAY VINAIGRETTE DRIZZLE

My love of oysters began the same day as my love of sushi. The oysters served in sushi restaurants are finished with slivers of carrot, daikon radish, rice vinegar and a splash of tamari or soy sauce. The combination of sweet rice vinegar and tart tamari, the texture of the vegetables and the brininess of the oysters is to me a perfect combination. My fondness for demi-sec Vouvray (semi-sweet Chenin Blanc from the Loire) and sherry vinegar inspired me to create this recipe, which flaunts the same combination with different ingredients.

RECOMMENDED WINE: drink what you cook with, Vouvray demi-sec (or other suitable bubbly)

JANET WEBB

SERVES 6

24–36	fresh oysters (Malpeques)	24–36
1	bottle Vouvray demi-sec	1
2 Tbsp.	good-quality sherry vinegar	30 mL
2	shallots, minced	2
1 Tbsp.	finely chopped fresh Italian parsley	15 mL
	kosher salt and freshly ground black pepper to taste	

Scrub the oysters and keep them cold until serving time. Place the wine in a small saucepan over medium heat, and simmer until it is reduced to $1/4$ cup (60 mL), about 30 minutes.

Once the wine is reduced, allow it to cool completely. Whisk the wine and the sherry vinegar together, add the shallots and parsley and season with salt and pepper.

Just prior to serving, shuck the oysters and plate them on the half-shell on individual beds of rock salt (this will help stabilize the oysters, so they don't move around). Drizzle each oyster with the vinaigrette and serve immediately.

GRILLED OYSTERS WITH BLOODY CAESAR SALSA

RECOMMENDED WINE: bubbly—as extravagant as champagne or as simple as prosecco

I am an oyster addict and while I like my oysters fresh, raw and straight up, I know that not everyone is quite so adventurous so I offer this easy way to lightly steam them. Grilled oysters take me back to an idyllic holiday in the California wine country—camping among the redwoods and slurping steamy fresh bivalves off the barbie. Oysters are made to grill. They steam to perfection in the shell and you don't have to bother with shucking. My clam-flavoured oyster sauce may be mixing apples and oranges, so to speak, but this spicy salsa (inspired by the Calgary invention, the Bloody Caesar) is great on oysters just off the grill. It's also perfect to spoon over raw oysters, just before slurping them out of the shell.

CINDA CHAVICH

SERVES 4

¼ cup	Clamato juice	60 mL
2	plum tomatoes, seeded and finely chopped	2
1	jalapeño pepper, seeded and minced	1
2 Tbsp.	vodka	30 mL
1 tsp.	fresh lime juice	5 mL
½ tsp.	celery salt	2.5 mL
	salt and freshly ground black pepper to taste	
1 dozen	large oysters in the shell	1 dozen
	celery leaves, for garnish	

Combine the Clamato juice, tomatoes, jalapeño, vodka, lime juice, celery salt, salt and pepper. Cover and refrigerate for at least 1 hour to meld the flavours.

When you are choosing oysters, make sure they are alive (and that the shells are tightly closed). Look for specimens that have a deep rounded base and flat top. It's easy to grill oysters—just set them on a hot grill, flat side up, and wait until they start to steam and then pop open. It takes about 5 to 10 minutes. It's easy to pry off the tops and saves you the challenge of shucking. Discard any oysters that don't open. Serve with the salsa.

SHRIMP WITH A COCONUT LEMON GRASS GLAZE

There is very little that cannot be improved with a splash of coconut. (For coconut milk, I like Thai Kitchen brand.) Use this compound butter on any fish or shellfish for an intense hit of Asian flavours. The lemon grass and kaffir lime leaves can be difficult to track down, but they can be kept frozen until you need them.

RECOMMENDED WINE: off-dry riesling from Germany

GAIL NORTON

SERVES 8 TO 10

2	14-oz. (398-mL) cans coconut milk	2
3 Tbsp.	minced lemon grass	45 mL
1 tsp.	minced fresh red chili	5 mL
1	kaffir lime leaf, very thinly julienned	1
2–3	limes, juiced	2–3
3 Tbsp.	fish sauce	45 mL
2 lbs.	shrimp, peeled, tails left on	950 g
1	bunch fresh cilantro, roughly chopped	1
5 Tbsp.	chopped fresh mint	75 mL
3	scallions, thinly sliced on the diagonal	3

In a non-stick heavy pot, bring the cream from the canned coconut milk to a boil. Reduce the heat to medium and cook until it is reduced by half. It should be a thick, white, creamy consistency. Add the lemon grass and red chili and cook at a vigorous simmer for about 5 minutes, or until the lemon grass has released its flavours. Add the lime leaf, lime juice and fish sauce and continue to simmer for about 5 minutes. At this point you should have about 1 cup (240 mL) of glaze.

Take a generous scoop of the glaze and add it to a frying pan (put enough in to cover the bottom of the pan). Heat until quite hot, then add the shrimp in a single layer. Cook the shrimp until they are slightly brown, flip and finish cooking. They are done when they are no longer opaque.

Remove the shrimp to a serving platter. Add more glaze to the pan and repeat. Do not clean the pan between batches—the browned bits have a pleasant nutty taste that adds flavour to the next batch.

Garnish with a sprinkling of cilantro, mint and scallions before serving.

Horseradish-Poached Shrimp

RECOMMENDED WINE: fruit-forward riesling from Canada or California

I have always experimented with the poaching liquid for shrimp. I first used freshly grated horseradish root and it was fantastic, but one time, unable to find fresh horseradish root, I tried the jarred variety and it translated very well. Go for the best horseradish in a jar you can find if no fresh horseradish is available. Horseradish does have a very strong smell and flavour, but because of the poaching method it merely permeates the shrimp with a nice, if different, bite.

MAKES ABOUT 40 TO 50 SHRIMP   KAREN MILLER

2 lbs.	shrimp, peeled and deveined (21 to 25 count) (see page 45)	900 g
1	8-oz. (227-mL) jar horseradish	1
1 Tbsp.	salt	15 mL
1	orange, juice and zest	1
1 Tbsp.	pickled ginger, slivered	15 mL
1 Tbsp.	pickled ginger juice	15 mL
1	jalapeño pepper, seeded and minced	1
	sea salt to taste	

Bring a large pot of boiling water to a boil. Add the shrimp, horseradish and salt. Cook on high until the shrimp are opaque and cooked through, about 3 to 4 minutes. Drain and serve warm or let cool and refrigerate to serve cold.

To make the dipping sauce combine the orange juice and zest, pickled ginger and juice and jalapeño pepper. Add a little sea salt if necessary.

SHRIMP IN FLAK JACKETS OF PROSCIUTTO & ROASTED GARLIC

You can never have too many shrimp at a party. Never. So arm yourself. Assemble the shrimp a day in advance, and pop them into a hot oven mere minutes before you want to share them. Smart hosts will circulate this dish themselves to ensure relatively even distribution among guests and shrimp fanatics. These ones need a warning label written in particularly large letters: "Addictive!"

RECOMMENDED WINE:
unoaked, fruity sauvignon blanc or Italian vernaccia di San Gimignano

DEE HOBSBAWN-SMITH   SERVES 4 TO 8

1 lb.	shrimp, cleaned and peeled (21 to 25 count) (see page 45)	450 g
4 oz.	chèvre	113 g
4	cloves roasted garlic, minced (see page 37)	4
3	sprigs fresh rosemary, finely minced	3
	freshly ground black pepper to taste	
13	thin slices prosciutto, sliced in half lengthwise	13
1 Tbsp.	olive oil	15 mL

Using a small knife, butterfly the shrimp lengthwise, slicing about halfway through. Mix together the chèvre, garlic, rosemary and pepper. Dab about $1/2$ tsp. (2.5 mL) of the mixture into the sliced pocket of each shrimp, wrap with a piece of prosciutto, and place on a parchment-lined baking sheet. When all the shrimp have been stuffed and wrapped, drizzle them with the olive oil, crack a little pepper over top, wrap well and refrigerate until needed.

When it's cooking time, preheat the oven to 425°F (220°C). Cook until the shrimp are pink and beginning to curl, about 5 minutes. Serve hot or at room temperature.

Thai Prawns with Toasted Sesame Seeds

RECOMMENDED WINE:
dry malvasia, fruity
Californian sauvignon
blanc or viognier

PRAWNS

The numbers preceding
the word "count" indicate
the number of prawns
per pound.

Judy Wood

Thousands upon thousands of prawns have been consumed because of this recipe. Toasted sesame seed oil is one of my favourite oils, but make sure you buy the smallest bottle. You only need a bit to do this well.

SERVES 6   JUDY WOOD

2 lbs	prawns, peeled and deveined (20 to 21 count)	900 g
2–3 Tbsp.	sesame seeds	30–45 mL
1	lime	1
3 Tbsp.	oyster sauce	45 mL
1 Tbsp.	soy sauce	15 mL
1	clove garlic, minced	1
1 Tbsp.	minced fresh ginger	15 mL
1 Tbsp.	chili paste	15 mL
2 Tbsp.	corn syrup	30 mL
2 Tbsp.	sesame oil	30 mL
1 Tbsp.	grated carrots	15 mL
1	green onion, sliced	1

Bring a pot of water to a boil. Add the prawns and cook for 3 to 4 minutes. Drain and allow to cool. To toast the sesame seeds, place in a dry pan over medium heat. Be sure to keep the pan moving, as once the oils begin to be released, browning occurs quickly.

Juice the lime into a bowl and add all the remaining ingredients.

When the prawns have cooled, add them to the marinade and allow to marinate for at least 10 minutes. To serve, place on a plate and sprinkle the sesame seeds over top.

GRILLED SCALLOPS WITH LEMON & ROASTED PEPPER RELISH

This was the dish that got me "Dishing." I prepared loads of it for a fundraising event and people were amazed that the relish contained the whole lemon, peel and all. The luxurious and creamy texture of a perfectly grilled scallop contrasts beautifully with the tart, rich flavour of the relish. Make sure you place the relish on the scallops while they are warm so they can absorb the flavour of the relish.

KAREN MILLER

MAKES 20 TO 30 PIECES, DEPENDING ON THE
SIZE OF THE SCALLOPS

2 Tbsp.	red wine vinegar	30 mL
1 Tbsp.	minced shallots	15 mL
1/2	lemon	1/2
1	red bell pepper, roasted and finely chopped	1
1 tsp.	capers, drained and chopped	5 mL
1/4 cup	olive oil	60 mL
	salt and freshly ground black pepper to taste	
1 lb.	large scallops	450 g
1 Tbsp.	olive oil	15 mL

Combine the vinegar and shallots and let stand for about 10 minutes. Cut 1/4 of the lemon into really thin slices and then chop those finely (removing any seeds) and add to the shallots. Add the roasted pepper, capers, olive oil and the juice from the remaining 1/4 lemon to the shallot mixture. Season the relish with salt and pepper.

Brush the scallops with olive oil and grill over high heat. If serving these as a passed appetizer, thread the scallops on skewers and pour the relish over top while still warm. They can also be plated up quite nicely—drizzle the relish around the plate for a beautiful colour presentation.

RECOMMENDED WINE:
Italian vernaccia or Loire muscadet

ROASTING PEPPERS

I roast my peppers on the flame of my gas element. Place them directly on a high flame and turn when blackened (They can also be done under the broiler of an electric stove.) Place the blackened peppers in a bowl and cover with plastic wrap. When cool, discard the stems and seeds and remove the blackened skin. This can be done a few days ahead. Drizzle them with a little olive oil and refrigerate.

KAREN MILLER

Sesame-Crusted Salmon Satés with Orange Ginger

RECOMMENDED WINE:
Californian viognier or
fruity, unoaked Australian
chardonnay

I borrowed this dish from Hugh Carpenter and tweaked it a bit.
I was thrilled to reduce the number of chicken satés out there
while still providing an easy and very tasty appetizer.

Makes 18 satés   Judy Wood

18	6-in. (15-cm) bamboo skewers	18
1	12-oz. (340-g) fillet salmon, skin removed	1
4 Tbsp.	oyster sauce	60 mL
2 Tbsp.	orange juice concentrate	30 mL
1 Tbsp.	soy sauce	15 mL
1	clove garlic, minced	1
1 Tbsp.	grated fresh ginger	15 mL
3 Tbsp.	chili paste	45 mL
4 Tbsp.	honey	60 mL
1 Tbsp.	sesame oil	15 mL
2–3 Tbsp.	toasted sesame seeds	30–45 mL

Presoak 18 bamboo skewers for at least 30 minutes.

Slice the salmon into thin strips. Weave the strips onto the
presoaked skewers and set them aside.

In a separate bowl combine the oyster sauce, orange juice
concentrate, soy sauce, garlic, ginger, chili paste, honey and
sesame oil, stirring thoroughly. (The marinade can be made
ahead of time and kept in the refrigerator.)

Brush half the marinade onto the salmon and let sit for
10 minutes. Heat the grill to medium. Grill the salmon for
1 to 2 minutes on each side. Brush the remaining marinade on
the cooked salmon and sprinkle with the toasted sesame seeds.

Smoked Salmon Tartare

A tartare dish usually involves raw meat or fish that is "cooked" by the other ingredients. This recipe plays on the technique of tartare instead. I have used the strong bursts of flavour from finely chopped shallots, capers, chilies and lime juice to complement the rich silky texture of the smoked salmon. I always tell people to serve this on the new olive oil potato chips that are available now. They come in great flavours (lemon, cracked pepper, rosemary) and fabulous colours (blue, red bliss). They are quite thick, so they hold up well to the salmon mixture.

RECOMMENDED WINE: sauvignon blanc/viognier blend from France

Karen Miller

Makes about 20 small servings

6 oz.	smoked salmon, diced	170 g
2 Tbsp.	capers, rinsed and chopped	30 mL
1	tomato, seeded and diced	1
1	shallot, diced	1
½ tsp.	sea salt	2.5 mL
½ tsp.	freshly ground mixed peppercorns	2.5 mL
½	lime, juice only	½

Combine all the ingredients and toss gently. Check the seasonings, adding more salt and pepper if necessary. Let it sit for about ½ hour before serving and check again for seasonings. You may have to add a little more lime juice.

Chicken Mango in Tortilla Cups

RECOMMENDED WINE:
nice, dry, light bubbly,
a dry riesling or light,
dry gewurztraminer

This is a very versatile recipe with which you can have some fun. It's great as is, but you can remove the chicken and make it vegetarian. Or add a variety of diced fresh fruit and leave out the sesame oil for a totally different and very fresh flavour.

MAKES 3 TO 4 DOZEN   JUDY WOOD

2	whole boneless skinless chicken breasts	2
3–4	fresh corn or flour tortillas	3–4
1/2	red bell pepper, finely diced	1/2
1	mango, finely diced	1
2	green onions, finely diced	2
1 tsp.	minced garlic	5 mL
2 tsp.	minced fresh ginger	10 mL
1 Tbsp.	oyster sauce	15 mL
1 tsp.	soy sauce	5 mL
1 Tbsp.	hot sauce	15 mL
2 Tbsp.	toasted sesame oil	30 mL
1 Tbsp.	chopped fresh cilantro or basil	15 mL
	salt and freshly ground black pepper to taste	

Preheat the oven to 350°F (175°C).

Heat the grill to medium-high and cook the chicken breasts for about 15 minutes, turning to brown all sides, until they are completely cooked. Set them aside to cool.

While the chicken is cooling, prepare the tortilla cups. Using a cookie cutter, cut the tortillas to fit into mini muffin tins. Bake for 10 to 15 minutes, or until they are lightly browned. Allow them to cool in the pan, then remove them and set aside to be filled.

Chop the cooled chicken into fine cubes and place in a bowl. Add the red pepper, mango and green onion. In a separate bowl, combine the garlic, ginger, oyster sauce, soy sauce, hot sauce and sesame oil. Blend well. Add the marinade to the chicken mixture and stir in the cilantro or basil. Let it marinate for at least 10 minutes before filling the tortilla cups. Fill the tortilla cups just before you are ready to serve them.

Mini Blini CORNETS Stuffed with COLD-SMOKED SALMON Mousse & Crystallized LEMON

Tiny, cute, do-ahead, and delicious. Perfect party food for the fiddly-minded. For the less fiddly, scoop the mousse into several pretty bowls and smooth the tops. Top it with roe and simply arrange the mini blini on a plate around the bowl.

DEE HOBSBAWN-SMITH

MAKES ABOUT 60 MINI BLINI CORNETS

1 lb.	cold-smoked salmon	450 g
1 lb.	plain cream cheese (firm, not spreadable)	450 g
1 Tbsp.	minced lemon zest	15 mL
1 Tbsp.	lemon juice	15 mL
1–2 Tbsp.	whipping cream	15–30 mL
2 Tbsp.	minced fresh chives	30 mL
1 Tbsp.	minced fresh thyme	15 mL
	pinch hot chili flakes or cayenne pepper	
1 recipe	Mini Blini	1 recipe
1/2 cup	salmon or flying fish roe, for garnish	120 mL
1 recipe	Crystallized Lemon, for garnish	1 recipe
	fresh dill sprigs, for garnish (optional)	

Finely purée the salmon in a food processor. Add the cream cheese and blend well, scraping the bowl down once or twice as needed. Add the lemon zest and juice, whipping cream, chives, thyme and chili flakes or cayenne. Pulse 2 or 3 times to blend, or stir in by hand. Chill until needed, but be sure to let the cold mousse stand at room temperature for at least 1/2 hour prior to use so it is piping consistency.

To assemble, fill a piping bag fitted with an open star tip. Lay a row of mini blini in front of you on a flat tray and pipe a smooth curl or round of mousse onto the centre of each, making it large at one edge and tapering off to a tail at the other edge. Pinch two sides of the crêpe up at an angle, so that the narrow end is completely closed and the fat end is completely open. It should look like a mini cornet. Decorate each mini blini with a tiny dollop of roe, a piece of crystallized lemon and a sprig of fresh dill. Cover and chill until serving time.

RECOMMENDED WINE: clean, crisp bubbly from the Loire or Italy, or a steely French Chablis

A CRÊPE ON EVERY PLATE

Crêpe batter will happily wait for you in the fridge for up to one week. Even better, crêpes of any size will await your pleasure for four or five days, well-wrapped, in the fridge, and virtually indefinitely in the freezer. Suddenly, entertaining unexpectedly is easy. Think of wonderfully quick late-night apple crêpes with friends, and suddenly simple brunch dishes for extra guests on Sunday mornings. A stack of these mini discs will transform into cute little cornets when you pipe a curl of smoked salmon mousse into their centre and fold the edges up.

DEE HOBSBAWN-SMITH

Mini Blini

MAKES SEVERAL HUNDRED 2-INCH (5-CM) CRÊPES (OR 24 6-INCH/15-CM CRÊPES)

COOKING CRÊPES

To make conventional-size crêpes, heat an 8-inch (20-cm) non-stick fry pan or crêpe pan. Add a tablespoon (15 mL) of batter and swirl it around the pan, spreading it quickly with the back of a spoon to thinly and evenly cover the bottom of the pan. Cook over medium-high heat for a minute, then flip the crêpe and cook briefly on the second side. Stack the finished crêpes on a plate, cool, wrap well and chill until needed.

3/4 cup	all-purpose flour	180 mL
4	eggs	4
1 cup	milk	240 mL
1 Tbsp.	poppy seeds	15 mL
	salt to taste	
1/4 cup	melted unsalted butter	60 mL

Mix together the flour and eggs, whisking well. Slowly add the milk and whisk to eliminate any lumps. Strain the batter though a fine mesh sieve and let it rest for at least 1/2 hour. Stir in the poppy seeds, salt and melted butter.

To make mini blini, heat a flat (not ridged) grill over medium heat. Lightly oil it if it requires oiling. Use a gravy ladle to spoon out a teaspoon of batter into a small circle about 2 inches (5 cm) in diameter. Fill the grill with blini. Flip each as they brown, and cook briefly on the second side. Transfer the blini to a parchment-lined tray. Stack them tidily. Cool, then wrap and chill or freeze until needed.

Crystallized Lemon

MAKES ABOUT 1/2 CUP (120 ML)

Use these tender bites of flavour as garnish on desserts, especially chocolate and fruit, on ice cream, with pork dishes, and as garnish for smoked salmon dishes. A little goes a long way, so be sparing . . . what you don't use today will keep indefinitely in its syrup!

1/2 cup	lemon zest, coloured part only, thinly sliced	120 mL
	cold water to cover	
1 cup	sugar	240 mL
	berry sugar, for rolling	

Put the zest into a small pot, cover with cold water and bring to a boil. Drain. Replace the water and repeat the process twice more. The third time, add the sugar and bring to a boil. Simmer the zest in the syrup until it is tender, adding more water as needed. Pour the zest and syrup into a small glass jar, cover and store at room temperature. For sugar-coated zest, dry the strands on a rack, then roll them in berry sugar.

Hot-Smoked Trout
with Caper Aïoli

Smoking your own fish is simpler than you might think. You can carry your wok outside and use the grill as your heat source in case of excess smoke. You can also opt for fruitwood or hardwood instead of tea—just don't use a soft wood like pine, which generates a toxic smoke. Choose a mild tea as a smoking agent for trout—I like experimenting with some of the green Japanese varieties, but I usually fall back on Russian Caravan or, for an extremely smoky taste, tarry Lapsang Souchong. Use the aïoli anywhere a mayo with gusto is needed, in pasta salad, with roasted flank steak, on sandwiches, even as a chunky dip for good, olive-studded breads or as garnish for crudités.

RECOMMENDED WINE: crisp, unoaked Canadian chardonnay or German "trocken" riesling

DEE HOBSBAWN-SMITH   SERVES 12

2 Tbsp.	minced fresh rosemary	30 mL
4	cloves garlic, finely minced	4
1 tsp.	fennel seed, cracked	5 mL
1	orange, zest only	1
2 Tbsp.	white peppercorns, cracked	30 mL
2 tsp.	olive oil	10 mL
2.2 lbs.	trout fillets	1 kg
¼ cup	granulated sugar	60 mL
¼ cup	loose black tea	60 mL
¼ cup	raw white rice	60 mL
1	loaf good-quality sourdough bread, preferably olive or herb-flavoured	1
1 recipe	Caper Aïoli	1 recipe
	lemon slices, for garnish	
	sprigs fresh fennel or dillweed, for garnish	

Blend together the rosemary, garlic, fennel seed, orange zest, peppercorns and olive oil. A mortar and pestle is most efficient, or you can mash it into a paste in a small bowl. Smear the mixture over the trout, covering all the flesh, and let stand while you ready the smoking apparatus.

To smoke the trout, line the bottom of a wok with a piece of foil about 6 inches (15 cm) square. Put the sugar, tea and rice onto the foil and mix it around. Place a wire rack in the wok, and position it so that it does not touch the tea mixture. Gently lay the herbed fish on the rack in a single layer. Put the lid on, then dampen and roll up two cloth kitchen towels. Lay the rolled towels in the crack between the lid and the wok, being sure to cover the gap all the way around.

Put the wok on its ring onto high heat and cook, covered, until the fish is just done, about 20 minutes. (You can turn off the heat and remove the rolled towels and lid to check whether it is done without compromising the smoking.) Once the fish is cool enough to handle, remove the skins and gently break the fish flesh into chunks.

Slice and toast the sourdough bread. Drop dollops of Caper Aïoli onto the toasted bread and top each slice with some smoked fish. Garnish with lemon slices and fresh herb sprigs.

CAPER AÏOLI

MAKES ABOUT 1 CUP (240 mL)

1	egg yolk	1
1 Tbsp.	grainy Dijon mustard	15 mL
	juice of $\frac{1}{2}$ lemon	
$\frac{1}{2}$ cup	vegetable oil	120 mL
2–3 Tbsp.	cold-pressed canola oil, or extra virgin olive oil	30–45 mL
2–3	green onions or a handful of chives, finely minced	2–3
1 Tbsp.	finely minced fresh rosemary	15 mL
$\frac{1}{2}$ cup	finely minced kalamata olives	120 mL
$\frac{1}{2}$ cup	capers	120 mL
	hot chili flakes to taste	
	salt to taste	

In a non-reactive bowl, whisk together the egg yolk, mustard and lemon juice. Slowly drizzle in the oil, whisking thoroughly as you do so to form an emulsion. Add the remaining ingredients, balancing the flavours at the end. Cover and chill.

TUNA TAPENADE on TOAST

This is the kind of instant tapas everyone needs in their reper-toire. You'll find everything you need in a well-stocked pantry. Serve it with fresh baguette or homemade toasts, or toss with hot short pasta for an instant sauce. Cold-pressed canola oil is a unique Alberta product from Highwood Crossing Farm—a deep golden, nutty oil they've dubbed Canada's answer to extra virgin olive oil. Feel free to substitute olive oil.

CINDA CHAVICH

MAKES 1½ CUPS (360 mL) TAPENADE

For the tapenade:

1 cup	pitted green olives or anchovy-stuffed olives	240 mL
1 Tbsp.	minced fresh garlic	15 mL
2 Tbsp.	cold-pressed canola oil or olive oil	30 mL
1	3½-oz. (100-mL) can tuna, packed in olive oil	1
1 tsp.	grainy mustard	5 mL
½ tsp.	hot pepper sauce	2.5 mL
½	lemon, juiced and zest minced	½
2 Tbsp.	chopped fresh parsley	30 mL

Combine the olives and garlic in a food processor and pulse until chopped but still chunky. Add the oil, tuna, mustard, hot sauce and lemon juice. Pulse again to combine.

Process for a few seconds. The tapenade should be pasty but still a little coarse. Add the lemon zest and chopped parsley and pulse just to combine. Refrigerate.

RECOMMENDED WINE:
dry, lively prosecco or fully dry pinot grigio from Italy

ANCHOVY-STUFFED OLIVES

You can buy cans of anchovy-stuffed olives in good grocery stores and Italian markets. Try them instead of regular pitted olives next time you shop. The anchovy is mild but adds that shot of salty umami to the olives that makes them especially addictive.

LEMON ZESTERS

Use a lemon zester to peel the zest of a lemon in thin strands, then chop the strands finely for this recipe. There is no other tool that can do the job of a good zester. Invest in a better quality, brand name model. The knock-offs really don't work and will just leave you frustrated.

For the toasts:

1	clove garlic, pressed	1
1/4 cup	good-quality olive oil	60 mL
1	baguette or French stick	1

Combine the oil and pressed garlic and let stand for 10 minutes to infuse. Slice the bread on the diagonal into thin slices and quickly brush each side with a little garlic oil. Place the bread in a single layer on a baking sheet. Bake at 400°F (200°C) for 2 to 3 minutes, or until just starting to turn golden brown. Cool and serve with the tapenade.

Provençal Tarts

This comes from one of my favourite regions in France. When I'm in need of some comfort, I often make this as one large tart and serve it with a light salad. The key ingredient is the herbes de Provence. If you want to make your own, you can get quite close by blending equal amounts of thyme, basil, savoury, fennel and lavender. Your local specialty shop will probably carry it already blended.

RECOMMENDED WINE: something from Provence of course!—a stunning rosé or herbaceous sauvignon blanc

JUDY WOOD

MAKES 3 TO 4 DOZEN TARTS

For the pastry:

2 cups	all-purpose flour	480 mL
2 tsp.	salt	10 mL
$1/3$ cup	cold butter, cut into pieces	80 mL
$1/3$ cup	water	80 mL

Place the flour and salt in a food processor and blend. Add the butter and blend until the mixture is crumbly. Add the water slowly and pulse the food processor to avoid overmixing. Remove it from the bowl and gently pat the pastry together into a disk. Wrap in plastic and let it rest in the refrigerator for at least 1 hour.

Roll the pastry out on a floured surface to a thickness of $1/8$ inch (.3 cm). Cut the pastry rounds to fit your tart pans and press the pastry into place. Let it rest in the refrigerator for another 15 minutes. While the pastry chills, make the filling.

For the filling:

3 Tbsp.	butter	45 mL
1	portobello mushroom, thinly sliced	1
1	shallot, sliced	1
3	Roma tomatoes, sliced	3
3–5	asparagus spears, sliced on the diagonal into 1-inch (2.5-cm) pieces	3–5
3 oz.	goat cheese, crumbled	85 g
1 tsp.	herbes de Provence	5 mL
½ cup	whipping cream	120 mL
1	egg	1
½ tsp.	salt	2.5 mL
½ tsp.	ground black pepper	2.5 mL

Preheat the oven to 375°F (190°C).

Melt the butter in a sauté pan over medium-high heat. Add the mushroom and sauté for about 5 minutes. Add the shallot and sauté for 5 minutes. Set the mixture aside to cool.

Combine the cooled mixture with the tomatoes, asparagus, cheese and herbes de Provence in a bowl. Blend the cream and egg together in a separate bowl.

Fill the tart shells to the top with the filling. Spoon the egg mixture over the filling. Bake the tarts for 20 to 25 minutes, until they are a golden brown.

These tarts freeze well. Let them cool completely before freezing. When you want to serve them, allow them to thaw first, then bake at 350°F (175°C) for about 5 to 7 minutes.

Beef Roulades with Cambozola Butter

This recipe has to be dedicated to Elspeth, who got me into the catering end of the food business. We have prepared millions of these rolls over the years and no one seems to tire of the ever-so-classic combination of great beef with creamy blue cheese. With the ever-increasing availability of peppery arugula leaves, this is one everyone can make for their next party. Keep a batch of Cambozola butter on hand in your freezer, and you'll find yourself making these all the time.

RECOMMENDED WINE: spicy, earthy Côtes du Rhône or other red from southern France

Karen Miller

Makes about 30 pieces

2 Tbsp.	soy sauce	30 mL
2 Tbsp.	canola oil	30 mL
4 Tbsp.	white wine vinegar	60 mL
1 lb.	beef tenderloin fillet	450 g
	salt to taste	
	freshly ground black pepper to taste	
8 oz.	Cambozola cheese, at room temperature	225 g
3 Tbsp.	unsalted butter, softened	45 mL
	freshly ground black pepper to taste	
30	arugula leaves (or watercress)	30

Combine the soy sauce, oil and vinegar in a non-reactive container. Add the beef and marinate for at least $\frac{1}{2}$ hour and up to overnight. Remove the beef from the marinade and salt generously. Heat the barbecue to high and grill all sides on the barbecue or in a grill pan, for about 1 minute each side.

Preheat the oven to 350°F (175°C). Pepper the beef generously, place it on a baking sheet or pan and bake for about 15 minutes more. Remove from the oven and let cool. When cool, refrigerate if time permits (it makes it easier to slice).

Prepare the Cambozola butter by combining the cheese, butter and pepper. Clean the arugula and trim the stems if necessary.

Slice the beef into thin slices. Place a spoonful of the Cambozola butter on a piece of beef and top with a piece of arugula. Roll it into a cone with the arugula sticking out.

ARTICHOKE &
ARUGULA PESTO

RECOMMENDED WINE:
Aperitif! Prosecco from
Italy, Spanish Cava or Alsace
Crement

I like this as a dip with crackers or baguette rounds, as a spread in a sandwich, or tossed with a little fresh pasta.

MAKES ABOUT 2 CUPS (480 ML)   PAM FORTIER

3	bulbs garlic	3
1	6-oz. (170-mL) jar marinated artichokes, drained	1
1/3 cup	extra virgin olive oil	80 mL
1/2 cup	grated Pecorino Romano cheese	120 mL
2 cups	packed arugula, washed, dried and thick stems removed	480 mL
	dash hot pepper sauce	
	salt and freshly ground black pepper to taste	

Preheat the oven to 350°F (175°C). Wrap the garlic in foil and roast for 1 hour. Cool. Squeeze the cloves out of the papery husks directly into the bowl of a food processor fitted with the metal blade. Add the remaining ingredients and process to a smooth paste.

MEXICAN GREENS QUESADILLAS WITH FRESH PINEAPPLE SALSA

I had the best quesadilla of my life at a restaurant in Phoenix. It was called a Mexican greens quesadilla and contained fresh ezpazote, which has quite an intense minty flavour. Not being able to find an easy fresh supply of this herb, I came up with this combination. In summer I make it with the organic mixed baby greens growing in my garden and get a wonderful fresh "green" taste sensation. If you want to try fresh ezpazote, look for it at Latin markets. They may only have the herb dried, in which case you could add a little to the fresh combination to get a feel for the very different flavour of ezpazote.

RECOMMENDED BEER/WINE: light, fresh lager or Spanish verdelho

KAREN MILLER

MAKES 40 MINIATURE QUESADILLAS

10	10-inch (25-cm) flour tortillas	10
1 cup	baby salad greens	240 mL
¼ cup	chopped fresh oregano	60 mL
¼ cup	chopped fresh marjoram	60 mL
	salt and freshly ground black pepper to taste	
8 oz.	queso fresco or Jack cheese (good Monterey Jack is okay), crumbled or grated	225 g
1 recipe	Fresh Pineapple Salsa	1 recipe

Cut the tortillas into small 2-inch (5-cm) rounds. Mix the baby salad greens with the oregano and marjoram. (You can use regular salad greens but they would have to be chopped slightly to make them a more appropriate size.) Season with salt and pepper.

Place a mound of greens in the centre of a tortilla round. Cover each round with a spoonful of cheese and place another tortilla round on top. Press down on the quesadilla with something heavy. Bake in a 375°F (190°C) oven until crispy and golden or cook on a griddle, turning when brown spots appear on one side. Serve with the salsa.

Fresh Pineapple Salsa

MAKES ABOUT 1 CUP (240 mL)

¼	ripe pineapple, cut into small dice	¼
1	jalapeño pepper, seeds removed and finely diced	1
1	shallot, peeled and finely diced	1
1	lime, juice only	1
	sea salt to taste	

Combine all ingredients in a bowl and let sit for ½ hour. Taste and adjust salt and lime juice if required.

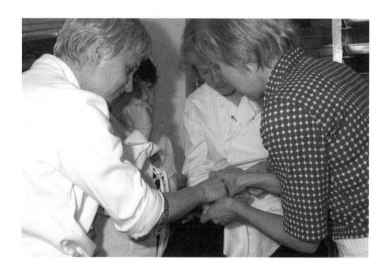

Arugula, Mint & Walnut Pesto for Pasta

This is a taste combination made in heaven: the pleasant bitter-ness of the walnuts is tempered with the mint, and the arugula adds a hint of pepper to the pesto. Make sure that the nuts are fresh. Use this pesto in place of the more common basil variety for a taste treat. For a variation, add a couple of roasted red peppers (see page 46) while blending, or use roasted hazelnuts instead of walnuts. Serve it as a plated first course or spread the pesto on crostini for a quick and delicious passed appetizer.

RECOMMENDED WINE:
white roussanne/marsanne blend from southern France

GAIL NORTON

Serves 4 to 6

3/4 cup	walnuts	180 mL
3 cups	arugula, thick stems removed	750 mL
1 cup	fresh mint, thick stems removed	250 mL
3	cloves garlic	3
1/4 cup	balsamic vinegar	60 mL
	olive oil	
1/4 cup	coarsely grated Parmesan or manchego cheese	60 mL
	salt and freshly ground black pepper to taste	
1 lb.	dried pasta (such as fusilli)	450 g

Toast the walnuts in a 375°F (190°C) oven until they are fragrant, slightly hot to the touch and lightly roasted, about 10 minutes.

Place the arugula and mint in a food processor and mince finely. Add the garlic and toasted walnuts, then the balsamic vinegar. With the machine running, begin adding the oil in a thin stream, using just enough to form a paste. Add the cheese, salt and pepper. Taste and adjust the seasonings.

Cook the pasta according to package directions in well-salted water. Drain, toss with the arugula pesto and serve immediately.

Piquillo Peppers Stuffed with Chèvre & Caramelized Cipollini Onions

RECOMMENDED WINE:
crisp albarino from Spain or a lighter tempranillo if red is desired

These Spanish peppers are a bit piquant, a bit delicious. Stuff them with whatever you will, plate them for a first course, pick them up in your fingers for a walkabout. If you cannot locate cipollini onions (check at Italian markets), use mild white onions, finely sliced. No piquillos in your store? Use roasted and peeled pasilla (or jalapeños if you have a taste for heat).

SERVES 10 TO 15   DEE HOBSBAWN-SMITH

1 lb.	cipollini onions	450 g
2 Tbsp.	butter	30 mL
2 Tbsp.	sherry vinegar	30 mL
	salt and freshly ground black pepper to taste	
	pinch fresh or dried thyme	
1	bulb roasted garlic (see page 37)	1
1 lb.	chèvre	450 g
1	12-oz. (565-mL) can piquillo peppers	1
	olive oil, for drizzling	

Cook the onions, butter, vinegar, salt, pepper and thyme in a shallow sauté pan until the onions are tender, 15 to 30 minutes. Keep the heat moderate to prevent burning. Cool the cooked mixture, then chop up the onions. Stir in the chèvre.

Preheat the oven to 450°F (230°C). Use a piping bag fitted with a plain tip to fill the piquillo peppers with the filling. Arrange the stuffed peppers in a single layer on a parchment-lined tray, drizzle with olive oil and bake until hot, about 10 minutes.

Nori Rolls with Grilled Vegetables & Chèvre

The key ingredient in this recipe is the rice, and very specific methods must be followed in order to achieve the perfect outcome. The proper ingredients are also important, so absolutely no substitutions please. The good news is that once you master making the rice, you really have as much creative licence as you wish with the selection of fillings. The rice, nori and sushi mats are available at Japanese specialty food stores.

RECOMMENDED WINE: fruity Australian semillon/sauvignon blend or similar from USA

SHELLEY ROBINSON   MAKES 4 SUSHI ROLLS (EACH ROLL CAN BE CUT INTO 10 SLICES)

2½ cups	Japanese sushi rice	600 mL
3¼ cups	water	780 mL
1 cup	rice wine vinegar	240 mL
⅓ cup	sugar	80 mL
2 Tbsp.	salt	30 mL
1 Tbsp.	mirin	15 mL
1 lb.	assorted vegetables for grilling (asparagus, red bell pepper, green onion, portobello mushrooms)	450 g
2 Tbsp.	olive oil	30 mL
1 Tbsp.	chopped garlic	15 mL
1 Tbsp.	chopped fresh thyme	15 mL
	salt and freshly ground black pepper to taste	
4	sheets nori	4
⅔ cup	crumbled goat cheese (about ½ lb./225 g)	160 mL
¼ cup	mushroom soy sauce	60 mL
1 Tbsp.	hot sauce	15 mL

Measure the rice carefully. Wash the rice in a large bowl under cold running water, while gently stirring it with your hand. Drain the water off as the bowl fills and repeat this process until the water you pour off is no longer milky but runs clear. Place the rice and water in a pot with a lid. Cover and cook over medium heat until it comes to a boil. As soon as it begins to boil, turn the heat to high for 1 minute. If the lid begins to bounce from the steam pressure, place something heavy on top to weigh it down. Turn the heat down to low and cook for 4 to 5 minutes, then reduce the heat to the lowest setting and cook for 10 minutes. Remove the rice from the heat and let stand for 10 minutes, covered.

Put the cooked rice into a wood or glass mixing bowl and spread it out in an even layer. Place the rice wine vinegar, sugar, salt and mirin in a bowl and mix until the sugar is dissolved. Sprinkle the vinegar mixture over the rice. Using a large wooden spoon, mix the vinegar into the rice with a slicing motion. If possible, have a helper fan the rice at the same time. Continue mixing and fanning until the rice is cool. Keep the sushi rice covered with a damp cloth at room temperature until ready to use.

Preheat the grill or barbecue to medium. Prepare the vegetables by washing and trimming as required. (For example, cut bell peppers in half and remove the seeds and stem. Asparagus just needs to be washed. For portobello mushrooms, remove the stem and scrape out the brown gills at the bottom of the cap.) Toss the prepared vegetables in the olive oil, garlic and thyme, season with salt and pepper and grill until tender. Remove the vegetables from the grill, cool and cut them into long thin slices.

Place one sheet of nori shiny side down on a sushi rolling mat. Have a bowl of cold water at your side to dip your hands into before touching the rice. Take about $\frac{1}{4}$ of the rice in your hand and carefully spread it as evenly as possible over the nori sheet, leaving a 1-inch (2.5-cm) strip uncovered by rice at the top of the sheet. Place $\frac{1}{4}$ of the vegetables and cheese in a strip across the rice, near the bottom edge. Roll the bottom edge of the mat up and over the ingredients so that the bottom edge of the nori is touching the rice on the other side of the filling. Press the mat to tighten the roll, then lift the bottom edge of the mat out of the way and complete the roll, ending up with the seam on the bottom. Press the mat around the roll to shape it. Repeat for the remaining rolls.

Mix the soy sauce and hot sauce in a dipping bowl or bowls. Use a sharp, thin-bladed knife to cut the rolls into slices. Dip the knife into water between each slice. To serve, arrange the slices on a platter with the dipping sauce.

Parmesan Tuiles with Basil Tomato Mousse

This recipe is based on a lovely little appetizer I tasted at the MGM Grande Hotel in Las Vegas. I was there for a food writer's convention and was impressed by the hors d'oeuvres they passed with champagne during a tour of The Mansions, private residences for high rollers.

Cinda Chavich

RECOMMENDED WINE: Champagne!

MAKES 16 TO 18 BITES

4 oz.	soft goat cheese	113 g
2 oz.	mascarpone or plain cream cheese	57 g
1 Tbsp.	sour cream or yogurt	15 mL
¼ cup	finely chopped sun-dried tomatoes packed in oil	60 mL
1 Tbsp.	basil pesto	15 mL
⅛ tsp.	freshly ground black pepper	.5 mL
1 cup	finely grated Parmigiano-Reggiano cheese	240 mL

In a food processor, combine the goat cheese, mascarpone or cream cheese, sour cream or yogurt, tomatoes, pesto and pepper. Purée until very smooth. Place the mousse in a piping bag with a plain narrow tip and refrigerate.

To make the tuiles, line a baking sheet with Silpat (silicone-coated baking fabric) or a piece of baker's parchment. Using about 2–3 tsp. (10–15 mL) of cheese per tuile, sprinkle the cheese in piles on the baking sheet. Spread with your fingers to form 2½- to 3-inch (6.2- to 7.5-cm) circles. You should have enough for about 16 to 18 rounds.

Preheat the oven to 325°F (165°C). Bake the tuiles for 5 to 8 minutes, until they are beginning to colour. Don't overbake. If the cheese is too brown and crisp, it will be difficult to roll. Wrap each round of cheese quickly around the handle of a wooden spoon to form a tube and set aside to cool. Tuiles may be made a day or two in advance and kept in an airtight container.

Just before serving, use the piping bag to fill each tube with tomato mousse.

Planning Ahead

I love to entertain, and do it often—usually every weekend. It might range from a Sunday night family dinner of 4 to 8 to casual cocktail affairs that wine and dine 20 to 30 people throughout an evening. My philosophy on entertaining is pretty mainstream: keep it simple if possible; prepare any items that can be refrigerated or frozen well in advance (i.e. ice creams, vinaigrettes, dry rubs and soups); make lists of products to be purchased; and create a detailed timeline of what needs to be accomplished, so that I can spend time with the guests. There is nothing more stressful than being unprepared and spending all night in the kitchen while everyone else has fun. Include the guests in last-minute food prep, or allow them to contribute something to the meal. I find some of the best dinner parties have been the "kitchen" variety, where the guests end up in the kitchen for at least part of the evening.

My entertaining usually follows the seasons and availability of fresh foods. There are lots of barbecues in the summer months, with plenty of herbs and greens fresh from the garden and fresh seasonal fruit for dessert. In the winter I like heartwarming bistro fare with fruit crisps and tarts to end the meal. As the number of guests increase, I serve interactive food, like fondue, sushi and do-it-yourself items.

I love to introduce new and unusual wines from my store at dinner parties, matching them to the appropriate food or including them in a recipe like Fresh-Shucked Oysters with a Demi-Sec Vouvray Vinaigrette Drizzle (page 40). I often start an evening with hors d'oeuvres and bubbly and finish off with port or after-dinner drinks like grappa and calvados.

Having water available throughout the meal is a must, as it cleanses the palate between courses and between wines. Your guests will also appreciate it when many wines may be consumed in an evening.

Also of importance: I like to set the table simply to allow the food to have the spotlight. Spend time polishing cutlery and glassware, as the quality of presentation is as important as the quality of the food. My choice of plates and bowls always takes into consideration the optimum presentation of the food being served. I have many different inexpensive styles of place settings, which allows me to have interesting variation throughout a meal (and keeps me out of the dish pit and at the table with my friends).

Entertaining is really all about spending precious time with friends and family. I like to make it easy on myself, so that my socializing time is maximized.

Janet Webb

67

My Tapas Parties

Food is my life, one might say. It's how I make my living, and it challenges me almost daily. When I am cooking I feel the most comfortable and in control, and my creativity has an outlet. Some people paint, some people sculpt. I cook—it is my art form. So trying to narrow the subject down to one favourite style or form of entertaining is difficult. But thinking back to some of my evenings with friends or family I realized that the times I enjoy the most are the evenings I call tapas parties. I can be creative with the cooking, but I also get to socialize while enjoying the food, company and wine. At a tapas party the dishes are served up all at the same time, in bowls and platters of varying shapes, sizes and colours. The wines have been carefully selected (with the help of a professional) to enhance the flavours chosen for the evening. When the food is on the table, the glasses have been filled to the appropriate level and your guests are buzzing with anticipation of the gastronomic fantasy that lies before them, you all sit down, together. The food is passed about with much discussion, the wine is tasted and opinions begin to emerge. The room is filled with people who are very important to you and you are down to the very basics of breaking bread together. What lies before you is a night of memories in the making. You don't have to get up and disturb the natural flow of the evening to get the second and third course ready. You are an active member of the group. There is that moment when you sit back and say to yourself, "It doesn't get much better than this," and you are proud that you were the instigator of this night. I wouldn't trade my tapas parties for anything.

Judy Wood

Party Dos and Don'ts

What is it about parties, dinner or not, that makes some memorable and others a disaster? Here are some of my own ideas on how (and how *not*) to entertain.

My biggest pet peeve is when the TV is on. The only exception to this rule is if you are having a Super Bowl party. If you're anything like me you experience what is commonly known as "TV face" and spend the entire time staring open-mouthed at the screen despite your best attempts not to. If someone wants to watch a sports event, they shouldn't accept the invitation in the first place. Isn't that what VCRs are for? Having said that, it is wise not to plan a party if you know that the Grey Cup finals are on.

Music is another big one for me. Ambient music is more than a nice touch—I consider it essential to setting the mood. I always notice when there is no background music playing. If you're unsure of what music is appropriate, have someone in the know put together a mixed disk or tape for you.

Another situation that may be difficult for guests is when the hosts are in the kitchen the whole time. A stressed host affects everyone, so do everything you can to let yourself join the fun when appropriate—at least try to make sure that you sit down and eat with your guests when it's time for dinner! Nobody will relax if you're in the other room already preparing dessert.

Here are a few more quick dos and don'ts. Always have plenty of alcohol on hand and don't assume everyone will bring a bottle of wine. Don't ask people to take their shoes off, regardless of the weather; shoes are often an integral part of a guest's outfit or, if you're like me, you've just slipped some shoes on with-out socks and feel awkward in bare feet. Do not make costume parties optional. There's nothing worse than having you and your date dressed as Tonya Harding and Nancy Kerrigan only to discover that you're the only ones in costume. Finally, if there are vegetarians in the group, be very careful not to mix up the serving spoons in dishes.

Rhondda Siebens

SECONDS

SOUPS & SALADS

Chorizo & Clam Soup

The secret to the amazing flavour of this soup is the long slow cooking of the onions—do not rush or scrimp on the time needed to cook them.

RECOMMENDED WINE: slightly chilled, fruity dolcetto from Italy or gamay from California

Gail Norton

Serves 4 to 6

4 Tbsp.	butter	60 mL
4 Tbsp.	olive oil	60 mL
3	large onions, sliced	3
6	cloves garlic, chopped	6
4	chorizo sausages	4
1	bunch parsley, minced	1
4 cups	veal or chicken stock	1 L
4 cups	fish stock	1 L
1	13-oz. (375-mL) can whole clams	1
4 lbs.	live clams, cleaned	1.8 kg

Melt the butter with the olive oil in a large heavy bottomed pot over medium heat. Add the onion and garlic and sauté until soft, about 10 minutes. Remove the chorizo casings and crumble the sausage into the onions. Stir in the parsley, cover the pan, reduce the heat and slowly simmer for 30 to 45 minutes with the lid on the pot. Add the veal and fish stocks and bring to a boil for at least 10 minutes. Add the canned clams along with the juice in the can, and the live clams. Cover and cook until the clams open. Discard any unopened clams. Serve immediately.

Double Oyster & Spinach Chowder

RECOMMENDED WINE:
a crisp herbaceous sauvignon blanc from France—perhaps a Pouilly Fumé or Sancerre

I created this recipe to use the pre-shucked oysters you can find in jars at the seafood shop. The puréed base of potatoes, oyster mushrooms and spinach lets you get away with using less cream (and fat) than usual. Oyster stew is traditional at Christmas time—with slivers of brilliant green spinach and red bell pepper, it's particularly festive.

SERVES 6   CINDA CHAVICH

1	bunch spinach	1
1 Tbsp.	butter	15 mL
1 Tbsp.	olive oil	15 mL
1	large onion, minced	1
6	medium oyster mushrooms, minced	6
1	large Yukon Gold potato, peeled and chopped	1
2 cups	fish or chicken stock	480 mL
1 pint	shucked medium oysters, chopped into large pieces, liquor reserved	480 mL
1/2 cup	whipping cream	120 mL
2 cups	1% milk	480 mL
	salt and freshly ground black pepper to taste	
6 Tbsp.	slivered roasted red bell peppers (see page 46)	90 mL
	sweet Hungarian paprika, for garnish	

Wash the spinach well in a large sink of water and squeeze it dry. Discard the stems, roll the leaves and cut into chiffonade. Set aside.

Heat the butter and oil together in a large saucepan over medium-high heat and sauté the onion for 5 minutes. Add the mushrooms, potatoes and half of the spinach and cook, stirring, for 5 minutes longer. Add the stock and reserved oyster liquor. Cover, bring to a boil and simmer on medium-low heat for 15 minutes, or until the potatoes are soft.

Add the cream and simmer for 2 minutes longer. Purée, using an immersible blender. When the mixture is very smooth, add the milk and reheat, just to a simmer. Stir in the coarsely chopped oysters. Cover the pan and cook on medium heat for 2 to 3 minutes, just until the oysters have plumped and curled around the edges. Stir in the remaining spinach and cook for 30 seconds, until the spinach turns brilliant green. Do not overcook.

Season with salt and pepper. Ladle into wide soup bowls. Top each with a tablespoon (15 mL) of red pepper and a sprinkle of paprika to garnish the plate.

SHIITAKE MUSHROOMS & SHERRY SOUP

There are many varieties of mushrooms out there to choose from but my favourites for this recipe are shiitake, chanterelles and portabello. If you use shiitake, as I have, ensure that the stem is tender. If it is not, remove it and use it in a stock or a sauce for that secret ingredient. I recommend you use a medium sherry as that will have the nutty flavour required for the perfect compliment.

RECOMMENDED WINE: Palo Cortado sherry, or a more simple white Burgundy

JUDY WOOD

SERVES 6

1	small bulb garlic	1
1/3 cup	butter	60 mL
3	onions, minced	3
4 lbs.	shiitake mushrooms, stems trimmed and brushed lightly to remove dirt	1.8 kg
2 tsp.	fresh thyme	10 mL
3/4 cup	sherry	180 mL
8 cups	chicken stock	2 L
4 cups	whipping cream	950 mL
	pinch salt and freshly ground black pepper	

Preheat the oven to 400°F (200°C).

Cut the top off the garlic bulb, exposing the cloves. Place on a piece of foil and drizzle with a little olive oil. Bake for 25 minutes. When cool enough to handle, squeeze the cloves of garlic from the husks.

Melt the butter in a large soup pot over medium heat. Add the onions and garlic cloves and sauté for 3 to 5 minutes. Add the mushrooms and thyme. Sauté for 15 to 20 minutes, until the mushrooms have browned.

Add the sherry to the pot and cook, scraping up any browned bits from the bottom. Add the chicken stock and whipping cream. Bring to a boil, reduce the heat and simmer for about 45 minutes. Season with salt and pepper and serve.

Bad Day Soup (Lentil Soup with Pancetta & Tomatoes)

RECOMMENDED WINE:
simple, off-dry riesling from
Germany or Alsace

This soup got its name from my son who was given a steamy bowl when he wasn't feeling well. I used to tell him it had magic powers to heal tummies and make flu bugs go away. It seemed to do the trick for just about any ailment. One day I commented that I had a headache, and he said I should have some "bad day" soup to make it go away. The name has stuck and this magical concoction has cured everything from heartache to hangover. Serve with a simple salad and rustic bread for dunking.

Serves 4

3 Tbsp.	olive oil	45 mL	Janet Webb
2 Tbsp.	finely chopped onion	30 mL	
2 Tbsp.	finely chopped celery	30 mL	
2 Tbsp.	finely chopped carrot	30 mL	
1 cup	dry white wine	240 mL	
½ cup	finely diced pancetta	120 mL	
1	14-oz. (398-mL) can whole Roma tomatoes, with juice	1	
½ lb.	French lentils, washed and drained	225 g	
4 cups	chicken, beef or vegetable stock	950 mL	
	kosher salt and freshly ground black pepper to taste		

Heat the olive oil in a heavy stockpot. Add the onion, celery and carrot and sauté over medium heat until soft and fragrant, 5 to 10 minutes, stirring occasionally. Add the wine and sauté for 5 minutes. Add the pancetta and sauté for another 2 minutes. Add the tomatoes and juice. Break up the tomatoes with a spoon as they cook on medium-low heat for 20 minutes. Add the lentils and sauté for 5 minutes. Add the stock, cover and simmer until the lentils are tender, approximately 30 to 40 minutes depending on the lentils. If the lentils absorb too much stock, add more to thin it out. Season with salt and pepper. Serve steaming hot and feel better!

Red Onion Soup with Goat Cheese Toasts

We all remember the steamy hot onion soup of the past with the gooey Swiss cheese floating on top. This is a takeoff on the classic, with a little refinement thrown in to please a dinner party crowd. Instead of stringy Swiss, we have delicate goat cheese on toasted croutons. The red onions also give a pleasing colour to the soup instead of the dull gold-brown variety of yesteryear. As a variation, I have occasionally used Gorgonzola on the toasts.

RECOMMENDED WINE: goat cheese and caramelized onions scream for pinot noir or pinot gris; a good Canadian baco noir would also be great

JANET WEBB

SERVES 4

4 Tbsp.	butter	60 mL
2 lbs.	red onions, thinly sliced	900 g
2	cloves garlic, minced	2
2 tsp.	finely chopped fresh thyme	10 mL
½ cup	dry red wine	120 mL
2 Tbsp.	port	30 mL
4 cups	vegetable or chicken stock	950 mL
	kosher salt and freshly ground black pepper to taste	
8	slices French baguette cut ½ inch (1.2 cm) thick	8
2 oz.	goat cheese, softened	57 g

Melt the butter in a heavy stockpot. Add the onions and sauté over medium heat until browned, approximately 20 to 30 minutes, stirring occasionally. Do not allow the onions to burn. Add the garlic and thyme and sauté for another 2 minutes. Add the red wine and port, increase the heat to high and cook for 10 minutes to reduce the liquids. Add the stock and bring to a boil. Cover and simmer over low heat for another 30 minutes. Season with salt and pepper.

Toast the bread slices under the broiler until lightly browned. Top with the goat cheese. Pour the soup into heatproof bowls. Top each bowl with 2 toasts and return to the broiler until the cheese is warm and slightly browned. Serve immediately.

Velvety Pumpkin Bisque with Chili Oil Drizzle

RECOMMENDED WINE:
French chardonnay
(Chablis) with good acidity,
or perhaps a Canadian
pinot gris or pinot blanc

This is a gorgeous soup to serve on a chilly autumn night. It can be the highlight of a simple weekday get-together or the prelude to a spectacular wine and food evening. Vegetarians and carnivores alike will love this full-flavoured, satisfying bowl of goodness.

SERVES 4   JANET WEBB

1	small (2$\frac{1}{2}$-lb./1.1-kg) pumpkin	1
2 Tbsp.	butter or olive oil	30 mL
1	medium carrot, grated	1
2	medium onions, diced	2
2	cloves garlic, minced	2
4 cups	vegetable stock	950 mL
1	medium tomato, diced	1
$\frac{1}{2}$ cup	sour cream	120 mL
	kosher salt and freshly ground black pepper to taste	
4 Tbsp.	sour cream, for garnish	60 mL
	store-bought chili oil	

Cut the pumpkin in half and scoop out the seeds. Peel the pumpkin and cut into 2-inch (5-cm) pieces.

In a heavy stockpot, melt the butter or oil. Add the onion, carrot and garlic and sauté over medium heat until soft and fragrant, approximately 10 minutes. Add the pumpkin and stock. Cover the pan and bring to a boil. Add the tomato. Reduce the heat and cook uncovered for about 30 minutes, or until the pumpkin is tender.

Purée the soup in batches in a blender until very smooth. Return the soup to the pot and blend in the $\frac{1}{2}$ cup (120 mL) sour cream over low heat. Season with salt and pepper.

To serve, ladle the soup into warm bowls, top with a small dollop of the remaining sour cream and drizzle with chili oil to taste. Serve immediately.

PUMPKIN Soup with MAPLE Syrup CARAMELIZED Croutons

I first encountered pumpkin soup when I lived in Australia years ago. Convinced that the Australians simply called a variety of our squash "pumpkin," I tried to recreate the taste using a variety of squashes after a horrific attempt using the garden-variety carving pumpkin. After finally discovering sweet pumpkin, I've decided that maybe the Aussies were right in the first place. I love serving pumpkin soup for Thanksgiving dinner as an alternative to the traditional pumpkin pie.

RECOMMENDED WINE: crisp Alsatian pinot blanc or riesling

RHONDDA SIEBENS

SERVES 6

2 Tbsp.	butter	30 mL
2 Tbsp.	olive oil	30 mL
3	medium onions, finely chopped	3
1 Tbsp.	ground cumin	15 mL
3 lbs.	sweet pumpkin, peeled, seeded and coarsely chopped	1.35 kg
2	apples, peeled, cored and coarsely chopped	2
4 cups	chicken stock	950 mL
	salt and freshly ground black pepper to taste	
1 recipe	Maple Syrup Caramelized Croutons	1 recipe

Heat the butter and oil in a heavy stockpot. Gently sauté the onion and cumin over low heat until the onion softens, approximately 30 minutes. When the onions are tender, add the pumpkin and apple. Add the stock, making sure it covers the pumpkin. Simmer over low heat until the pumpkin is tender, approximately 25 to 30 minutes.

Strain the soup, reserving the liquid, and purée the solids in a food processor. Add some of the reserved liquid and process again. Return this mixture and the remaining liquid to the pot. (Alternatively, a hand-held blender is a fast and easy way to purée without having to transfer liquids.) Season with salt and pepper. Heat through and serve immediately, garnishing each bowl with the croutons.

Maple Syrup Caramelized Croutons

Makes about 1½ cups (360 mL)

½	small loaf ciabatta	½
⅓ cup	butter	80 mL
¼ cup	maple syrup	60 mL

Cut the bread into ½-inch (1.2-cm) cubes. Melt the butter in a large skillet. Add the maple syrup, heat it through and then add the bread cubes. Sauté over medium heat, stirring and tossing until browned.

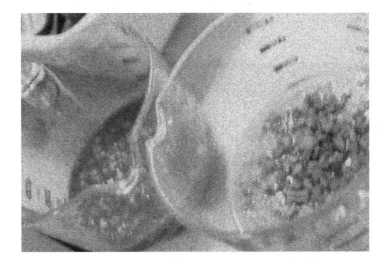

Chestnut Ravioli in Roasted Pumpkin Broth

This is my version of a wonderful pumpkin consommé with chestnut ravioli that I enjoyed at the Four Seasons Hotel in Vancouver. My thanks go to Chef Fabrice Rossmann for his inspiration. Using won ton wrappers, available at Asian markets, makes the ravioli quick and easy. Try roasting a variety of vegetables for the broth—regular Halloween pumpkin is the basis for this one.

RECOMMENDED WINE:
soft earthy Italian dolcetto or barbera or Canadian pinot noir

CINDA CHAVICH

SERVES 6 TO 8

For the broth:

1	5-lb. (2.25-kg) pumpkin, seeds removed and cut into large chunks	1
1	large yellow onion, coarsely chopped	1
2	large carrots, cut into chunks	2
1	small bulb fennel or 3 stalks celery, chopped	1
6	cloves garlic, unpeeled	6
8	medium brown mushrooms, halved	8
2–3 Tbsp.	olive oil	30–45 mL
2	sprigs fresh thyme	2
1 tsp.	whole black peppercorns	5 mL
1	bay leaf	1
1 tsp.	salt	5 mL
12 cups	cold water	3 L
1/4 cup	Amontillado sherry or cognac	60 mL
	salt and freshly ground black pepper to taste	

ROASTING AND PEELING CHESTNUTS

To roast chestnuts, cut an X in the bottom of each nut. Arrange in a shallow roasting pan and roast at 400°F (200°C) for 15 to 20 minutes, until the shells begin to curl. While the chestnuts are still warm, remove the shells and the bitter inner brown skin. If the skins are hard to remove, toss the peeled chestnuts in boiling water for an extra minute or two. Refrigerate the shelled nuts in a covered container, or freeze them for up to 3 months.

While I love the toasty flavour of freshly roasted chestnuts, Gail says it's far too much work. She advises buying canned or roasted vacuum packed chestnuts at specialty shops.

CINDA CHAVICH

To make the broth, toss the pumpkin, onion, carrots, fennel or celery, garlic and mushrooms with the olive oil in a shallow roasting pan. Preheat the oven to 400°F (200°C) and roast the vegetables for 1 hour, turning occasionally, until the vegetables are nicely browned. Reserve 1/2 cup (120 mL) of the roasted pumpkin for the ravioli.

In a large stockpot, combine the remaining roasted pumpkin and vegetables, thyme, peppercorns, bay leaf, salt and water. Bring to a boil over high heat, then lower the heat to medium-low and simmer for 1 to 2 hours.

Strain the broth through a colander and then through a fine sieve lined with cheesecloth to clarify. Reserve 1/4 cup (60 mL) of the broth for the ravioli. Return the remaining broth to a saucepan and simmer for 45 minutes over medium heat to reduce and concentrate the flavours. Stir in the sherry or cognac. Season with additional salt and pepper.

For the ravioli:

1 cup	peeled and roasted chestnuts	240 mL
1 cup	vegetable stock	240 mL
2	sprigs fresh thyme	2
2 Tbsp.	butter	30 mL
¼ cup	minced onion	60 mL
1	clove garlic, minced	1
3 Tbsp.	cream cheese	45 mL
½ cup	reserved pumpkin	120 mL
	salt and freshly ground black pepper to taste	
1	12-oz. (340-g) package won ton wrappers	1
6–8	sprigs fresh thyme, for garnish	6–8

Combine the chestnuts with the stock and thyme in a saucepan. Bring to a boil over high heat, reduce the heat to medium and simmer for 5 minutes, until the chestnuts are soft. Strain and discard the thyme. Mash the chestnuts.

In a small sauté pan, melt the butter and sauté the onion and garlic over medium heat until it begins to brown. Set aside.

In a food processor, purée the cream cheese and reserved pumpkin until smooth. Add the chestnuts and pulse to chop coarsely. Add the cooked onion and butter and pulse to combine, using the reserved broth if the mixture is too stiff. Season with salt and pepper and set aside.

To make the raviolis, lay 6 won ton wrappers on a clean surface and cover the remaining wrappers with a damp towel so they won't dry out. Place 2 tsp. (10 mL) of the chestnut filling on each wrapper. Using a pastry brush, brush the edges of the won tons with water and set a second wrapper on top, pressing around the filling to seal. Cut away the excess pastry to form small squares or use a 2-inch (5-cm) round scalloped cookie cutter to trim each ravioli. As you finish the raviolis, set them in a single layer on a baking sheet lined with parchment. Cover with plastic until ready to cook (they can be refrigerated for up to 4 hours).

Cook the raviolis in a large pot of salted, boiling water until just tender and floating, about 3 to 5 minutes. Remove with a slotted spoon and arrange 6 to 8 raviolis in each of six shallow soup bowls.

Ladle some of the hot pumpkin broth over the raviolis and garnish with a sprig of fresh thyme.

THAI COCONUT NOODLE SOUP WITH SCALLOP ROSES & PRAWNS

I developed this recipe for a special dinner party—a gourmet dinner with a Southeast Asian theme. While some of the ingredients are a little exotic, you will find them all in an Asian grocery store. You can use shrimp only (increase the amount to 1 lb./450 g) to make this soup even easier, but the intricately cut scallops that blossom as they poach (a technique I learned from Palliser Hotel chef Takashi Ito) are beautiful and a real conversation starter.

RECOMMENDED WINE: Alsatian gewurztraminer or California viognier

CINDA CHAVICH

SERVES 4 TO 6

¼ lb.	rice noodles	113 g
½ lb.	large Canadian scallops (1 per person)	225 g
1	stalk lemon grass, white part only, bruised	1
6 cups	chicken stock	1.5 L
3	kaffir lime leaves	3
1 Tbsp.	minced fresh ginger	15 mL
1	clove garlic, minced	1
3 Tbsp.	lime or lemon juice	45 mL
2 Tbsp.	fish sauce	30 mL
2 Tbsp.	light soy sauce	30 mL
1	Thai or serrano chili, chopped	1
1 tsp.	brown sugar	5 mL
1	14-oz. (398-mL) can unsweetened coconut milk	1
½ lb.	large shrimp, peeled and deveined	225 g
1	large carrot, shredded or finely julienned	1
2	green onions, cut into 2-inch (5-cm) pieces and shredded	2
¼ cup	chopped cilantro	60 mL
½ cup	chopped Thai basil	120 mL
1	lime, cut into 8 wedges	1

Place the rice noodles in a bowl and pour boiling water over them to soften. Let soak for 15 minutes, then drain and set aside.

To make the scallop roses, set each large plump scallop on a cutting board between two parallel toothpicks or bamboo skewers. Using a sharp knife, cut each scallop in thin slices in one direction almost through to the base, using the skewers to prevent the knife from cutting entirely through the scallop. Repeat the slicing at right angles and set aside.

To make the soup base, remove the hard green stalks from the lemon grass and whack the white portion with the back of a chef's knife to bruise and release the oils. In a large saucepan, combine the lemon grass, stock, kaffir lime leaves, ginger, lime or lemon juice, fish sauce, soy sauce, chili and sugar. Bring to a boil and simmer for 5 minutes.

Stir in the coconut milk and return to a boil. Add the shrimp, reserved rice noodles and carrot and simmer for 2 minutes. Add the scallop roses to the pan and simmer for 1 minute longer, just until they open like a flower. Discard the lemon grass.

Divide the noodles among the serving bowls, making a nest in which to nestle the single scallop rose. Pour the remaining soup around the edges of the bowl, and sprinkle with green onions, cilantro and basil. Serve with lime wedges to squeeze over top.

SPINACH, LEMON & THYME SOUP

I love soup. I love making soup. But sometimes I don't have the time or energy that is required. This recipe is great because the main ingredients, spinach purée and stock, can be made ahead and frozen—just thaw them in the microwave.

RECOMMENDED WINE:
herbaceous unoaked
sauvignon blanc
or malvasia

SHELLEY ROBINSON

SERVES 4

3 lbs.	fresh spinach, washed and stems removed	1.35 kg
6 cups	rich chicken or vegetable stock	1.5 L
4	lemons, washed	4
4	large eggs	4
2 Tbsp.	chopped fresh thyme	30 mL
1 cup	grated Parmesan cheese	240 mL
½ cup	dry Marsala	120 mL
	salt and freshly cracked black pepper to taste	

Heat a large pot of water to boiling. Plunge the spinach in all at once and stir. Allow the water to come back to a full boil, 2 to 3 minutes, before draining the spinach and rinsing it in cold water until it has completely cooled. Leave the spinach in the strainer and press some of the water out so it is moist but not dripping. Place the spinach in a food processor or blender and purée until smooth, stopping to scrape down the sides. (At this point the spinach can be frozen for another day.)

Bring the stock up to a boil, then reduce to a simmer. Remove the zest from the lemons, chop it finely and put in a medium bowl. Cut the lemons in half and remove the seeds. Squeeze out the juice and reserve.

Add the eggs, thyme, cheese and spinach purée to the zest and whisk to combine.

When you are ready to serve the soup, quickly whisk the blended ingredients into the lightly boiling stock. Add the wine, squeeze in the fresh lemon juice, season with salt and pepper, and serve. Because of the eggs, this soup will not hold or reheat, but it is fast to make. For a nice presentation, garnish with a scattering of edible flower petals.

LENTIL SALAD WITH MINT, ROASTED PEPPERS & FETA CHEESE

RECOMMENDED WINE:
soft, fruity beaujolais
or pinot noir

Usually lentils are associated with heavy, stewy dishes, but combining them with fresh, light flavours like mint and fruit juices takes them to a new level. The feta cheese lends a lovely creaminess to this dish; you could replace it with one of your favourite cheeses. Du Puy lentils are a French variety that is highly regarded because of the chewy texture—even with prolonged cooking they stay intact in their jackets. You can use any brown or green lentil, but stay away from orange lentils, which cook down to a mush and are not intended for use in salads.

SERVES 6 TO 8   GAIL NORTON

1 cup	lentils (preferably French du Puy lentils)	250 mL
2	red bell peppers, roasted, peeled and coarsely chopped (see page 46)	2
1	medium carrot, peeled and diced	1
½	small onion, finely chopped	½
1	clove garlic, finely chopped	1
3 Tbsp.	chopped fresh mint	45 mL
3 Tbsp.	chopped fresh parsley	45 mL
3 Tbsp.	chopped fresh cilantro	45 mL
⅓ cup	red wine vinegar	80 mL
8 oz.	feta cheese, crumbled	225 g
1	large lemon, juice and zest	1
	pinch paprika	
	pinch cayenne	
¼ cup	olive oil	60 mL
	salt and freshly ground black pepper to taste	

Rinse the lentils. Place them in a saucepan, cover them with water and bring to a boil. Turn down the heat and gently simmer until the lentils are tender, about 20 to 30 minutes. They should still be firm and holding their shape. Drain. Combine all the ingredients in a salad bowl and gently stir. Taste and season with more salt and pepper if needed.

GRILLED CAESAR SALAD WITH MINTED DRESSING & PARMESAN CHIPS

In Calgary, the barbecue is an obvious extension of the kitchen in the summer months. But I use the barbecue all year round and find that when it's 25° below (-32°C), the smell and taste of grilled food is really uplifting. This salad will impress your guests, both in taste and presentation. Try it as a starter to a hearty beef dish.

SHELLEY ROBINSON

SERVES 4

RECOMMENDED WINE: slightly chilled gamay beaujolais or slightly oaked New World chardonnay

2	heads romaine lettuce	2
3	cloves garlic	3
2	anchovy fillets	2
1 Tbsp.	Dijon mustard	15 mL
2	medium eggs	2
2	lemons, juice and zest	2
1/2 cup	fresh mint leaves	120 mL
1 Tbsp.	sugar	15 mL
2 cups	olive oil	480 mL
	salt and freshly ground black pepper to taste	
1/2 cup	finely grated young Parmesan cheese	120 mL
2 Tbsp.	olive oil	30 mL

Trim away any bruised or torn outside leaves from the romaine. Cut each head in quarters lengthwise and trim half of the core away, leaving enough so that the leaves stay together. Plunge the romaine pieces into a large sink filled with cold water and push them under, holding the section by the core and moving it quickly back and forth to force water into the core end. Remove the section, core side up, and allow to drain. For very dirty lettuce this procedure may need to be repeated several times.

Place the garlic, anchovies, mustard, eggs, lemon juice and zest, mint leaves and sugar in a food processor or blender, and process to combine. With the machine running, slowly drizzle in the 2 cups (480 mL) olive oil. Season to taste with salt and pepper. Refrigerate until ready to use.

PARCHMENT AND SILPAT

To prevent foods from sticking and make for easy clean up, there are two great products available. Parchment paper comes in rolls or precut sheets and is available in some supermarkets and at kitchen supply stores. You trim the paper to fit the inside of a baking sheet or baking pan. It can be reused, provided the items baked are not too gooey. Silpat is a silicon material that is totally heat resistant. It is available in various sizes and can be purchased at kitchen supply stores. It is washable and reusable.

SHELLEY ROBINSON

Preheat the oven to 325°F (165°C). Line a baking sheet with parchment paper or Silpat, and place 2 tsp. (10 mL) of the grated Parmesan cheese in a corner. Using your fingertips, spread it out to a 2-inch (5-cm) circle. Repeat the process, allowing room between each circle, until you have 12 cheese circles. Bake, watching carefully, for about 10 minutes, or until golden brown. Remove and cool on the sheet until ready to use.

Preheat the grill to high. Drizzle the washed and drained romaine sections with the 2 Tbsp. (30 mL) of olive oil and season with salt and pepper. Place the sections on the hot grill and allow the romaine to brown on all sides. The grill will likely flare up as the oil drips on the flames; use tongs to keep the sections turning as this occurs.

To serve, put a little of the dressing on each plate, place a section of romaine on the dressing and spoon some of the dressing over top. Lean another romaine section up against the bottom piece in the 3 or 9 o'clock position. Spoon some more dressing over the top piece and garnish with 3 Parmesan chips on each plate.

Haricot Vert Salad with Figs & Walnut Vinaigrette

The direct translation of *haricot vert* is green bean, but the French version is thinner and slightly more intensely flavoured. Paired with the walnuts, they are divine.

RECOMMENDED WINE: Spanish white such as a viura (macabeo)

Gail Norton

Serves 6 to 8

1 lb.	haricots verts, tipped and tailed	450 g
2 Tbsp.	sherry vinegar	30 mL
	kosher salt	
3 Tbsp.	walnut oil	45 mL
1 Tbsp.	olive oil	15 mL
2 Tbsp.	minced green onion	30 mL
2 Tbsp.	minced fresh parsley	30 mL
1 Tbsp.	finely minced shallot	15 mL
6	large figs, stemmed and quartered	6
20	basil leaves, torn into large pieces	20
2 Tbsp.	coarsely chopped toasted walnuts (see page 93)	30 mL

Bring a large pot of water to a boil and add a large pinch of salt.

Drop the beans into the boiling water and cook at a full boil until they are slightly tender and cooked through, about 6 to 8 minutes. Drain, then rinse with cold water to stop the cooking process.

Combine the sherry vinegar, salt, walnut oil and olive oil in a large mixing bowl. Whisk vigorously. Add the green onion, parsley and shallot and mix well. Add the cooked beans, figs, basil leaves and walnuts to the bowl and toss gently and serve.

Prawn & Scallop Salad
with Tarragon Dressing

RECOMMENDED WINE:
a herbaceous sauvignon
blanc or muscadet from
the Loire; balancing may
be required

Blanching is the key to success here—it allows the texture of
the vegetables to balance the texture of the seafood and retains
the fresh colours that make this dish spectacular. Terrific for a
summer feast.

SERVES 4   JUDY WOOD

12	prawns	12
12	scallops	12
1/2 lb.	snow peas	225 g
2	carrots, sliced into rounds 1/8-inch (.3-cm) thick	2
1/4 cup	red wine vinegar	60 mL
1 Tbsp.	sugar	15 mL
1	clove garlic, minced	1
1 tsp.	Dijon mustard	5 mL
1/2 tsp.	tarragon	2.5 mL
1/2 cup	olive oil	120 mL
	salt and freshly ground black pepper to taste	

Bring a pot of water to a boil, add the prawns and scallops and
cook for 5 minutes only. Blanch the snow peas in another pot of
boiling salted water for 1 minute. Remove and place in a bowl
of water with ice to stop them from cooking. Repeat with the
carrots, but blanch them for 3 minutes.

In a separate bowl, combine the vinegar, sugar, garlic,
mustard and tarragon. Add the olive oil in a fine stream,
whisking constantly. Season with salt and pepper. Combine
all the ingredients in a bowl and serve immediately.

WATERCRESS, KUMQUAT & PINE NUT SALAD WITH CHAMPAGNE VINAIGRETTE

This salad is simply beautiful and beautifully simple. It makes a spectacular presentation for an elegant dinner party, and its fresh clean ingredients are the perfect foil for a heavy menu. Watercress is often difficult to find unless you grow it in your own backyard, but if by chance you find it, grab it—even if only for a refreshing midweek dinner. Other greens can be substituted with great success. I have used spinach, arugula and even blanched asparagus. For a slightly different tilt on the taste, use walnut oil and walnuts, or hazelnut oil and hazelnuts, instead of the olive oil.

JANET WEBB

SERVES 4 AS AN APPETIZER OR 2 AS AN ENTRÉE

4 cups	watercress, cleaned	950 mL
½ cup	pine nuts	120 mL
1 cup	kumquats, thinly sliced and seeded	240 mL
¼ cup	champagne vinegar	60 mL
½ cup	olive oil	120 mL
	kosher salt and freshly ground black pepper to taste	

Break or tear the watercress (or other greens) into bite-size pieces. Toast the pine nuts in a heavy skillet on medium-high heat until just brown. Allow the nuts to cool.

Combine the watercress, pine nuts and sliced kumquats in a bowl. Whisk the vinegar into the oil, and season with salt and pepper.

Toss the dressing with the other ingredients. Serve immediately on chilled plates.

Salad Towers of Slow-Roasted Tomatoes, Prosciutto, Parmesan & Greens

RECOMMENDED WINE: as the acidity in this salad is quite low, you could serve a crisp white, such as sauvignon blanc or dry riesling

This salad makes an impressive appetizer because of its rather dramatic presentation. It's very easy to prepare and can be done over a few days, with only the final assembly to do on the day of the dinner. I prefer to use arugula as the green because its peppery quality balances the intense flavours of the tomatoes and prosciutto, but I have used baby spinach with excellent results.

SERVES 6 AS AN APPETIZER OR 4 AS AN ENTRÉE   JANET WEBB

12	slices prosciutto, not too thinly sliced	12
12	Roma tomatoes, halved vertically	12
	kosher salt and freshly ground black pepper to taste	
1 Tbsp.	finely chopped fresh thyme	30 mL
1/4 cup	olive oil	60 mL
3 Tbsp.	balsamic vinegar	45 mL
3 Tbsp.	olive oil	45 mL
	kosher salt and freshly ground black pepper to taste	
2 cups	fresh arugula or baby spinach leaves	480 mL
12	curls Parmesan cheese, shaved with a vegetable peeler	12
1/4 cup	fresh basil leaves cut in a chiffonade, for garnish	60 mL

Preheat the oven to 350°F (175°C). Cut the prosciutto slices in half (into 5-inch/12.5-cm pieces). Place the prosciutto and tomatoes, cut side up, on a baking sheet. Season the tomatoes with the salt, pepper and thyme. Drizzle the 1/4 cup (60 mL) olive oil over the tomatoes and prosciutto. Bake for approximately 25 to 30 minutes, or until the tomatoes are soft and the prosciutto is crispy. Allow both to cool completely.

Prepare the vinaigrette by slowly whisking the balsamic vinegar into the 3 Tbsp. (45 mL) olive oil so that it emulsifies. Season with salt and pepper.

To serve, place 2 slices of prosciutto on the plate, top with some of the greens and top that with 1 tomato (2 halves). Add another 2 slices of prosciutto, then some more greens, then another tomato and then top with a few more greens. Place a couple of Parmesan shavings on top of the greens and then a sprinkling of basil. Drizzle some of the vinaigrette over the towers once they are all assembled. Serve immediately.

My Favourite Asparagus Salad

My version of this recipe was inspired by a famous Nantucket Island chef's idea of her very favourite way of having asparagus. I have clients who claimed they would never eat asparagus until they tasted it this way. The trick is not to overcook the asparagus (it does continue cooking after you drain it) and to put the dressing on it while it is hot, so that some of the dressing is absorbed. This is a great recipe for serving guests because you can let it sit for an hour and it will only improve. Make it in large quantities for a buffet platter or as an easy, prepare-ahead first plate of a spring or summer dinner menu.

RECOMMENDED WINE: crisp sauvignon blanc from France

KAREN MILLER

SERVES 4 TO 6

2 lbs.	asparagus, trimmed and peeled	900 g
1 Tbsp.	salt	15 mL
2 Tbsp.	balsamic vinegar	30 mL
2 tsp.	Dijon mustard	10 mL
2 tsp.	garlic, minced	10 mL
1/3 cup	olive oil	80 mL
	sea salt and freshly ground black pepper to taste	
2	ripe plum tomatoes, diced	2
1/2 cup	Parmesan cheese, freshly grated	120 mL

Bring a large pot of water to a boil. Add the asparagus and salt and blanch the asparagus. Cook until it's still crisp, about 3 minutes. Drain and arrange on a platter.

Make the dressing by whisking the vinegar, mustard, garlic and olive oil together. Season with salt and pepper and add the diced tomatoes. Pour over the warm asparagus and sprinkle with the Parmesan cheese.

Note: If you peel the bottom portion of the asparagus spears, you will have a very beautiful presentation of the different colours of the cooked asparagus. It looks great with the tomatoes in the dressing and is well worth the effort.

WALNUT SALAD

RECOMMENDED WINE:
since there is no vinegar,
this would be lovely with a
light, crisp riesling

NUTS AND NUT OILS

Nuts and nut oils can
become rancid quite
quickly and are best if
used as soon as possible.
Walnuts seem to be
especially prone to this,
and I am convinced that
the reason most people
say they don't like them is
that a lot of the walnuts
we get are already stale,
and hence bitter. Store
nuts and nut oils in the
refrigerator or freezer.
Keep nuts well wrapped to
prevent transfer of other
flavours.

Bring out the flavour of
nuts by toasting them.
Spread them on a baking
sheet and toast for 7 to
10 minutes in a 300°F
(150°C) oven. Use your
nose; they are done when
they are fragrant.

PAM FORTIER

This recipe is incredibly simple but uncompromising in its
ingredients. I usually make this salad in the fall when I can get
fresh walnuts in the shell from a local organic store. The time it
takes to shell the nuts is worth it for the flavour. Purchase oil
and nuts from shops with a good reputation and a rapid turnover, to ensure the oil is not already rancid when you buy it.

SERVES 4   PAM FORTIER

6 cups	arugula or mesclun greens, washed and dried	1.5 L
3–4 Tbsp.	walnut oil	45–60 mL
	sea salt (Maldon's is especially good) to taste	
½ cup	fresh walnuts, lightly toasted and cooled	120 mL

Place the greens in a salad bowl. Toss with the oil, using the larger quantity if necessary; the greens should be lightly coated.
Season with salt, starting with a little and adding more if required.
Divide among 4 plates and sprinkle with the walnuts, crushing
them lightly in your hands.

The Storm Before the Calm

Picture a beautiful summer day for an all-day (and night) celebration for your closest 150 friends. No expense has been spared. Right down to flying in live trout to stock your pond so the children can fish for dinner later that day.

Behind the scenes a completely different story is unfolding. The delivery vehicle starts to pull out of the loading dock. There is a very steep angle to the ramp. The people who have loaded the vehicle have forgotten to tie things down and close the doors. The vehicle starts up the ramp and the loading dock floor is decorated with the beautiful colour smatterings of approximately 500 assorted desserts. It's only 6:15 a.m. The terrific staff begin to prepare all new desserts and the day begins again.

We are at the beautiful location for this great event and things seem to be going along swimmingly. (Nice segue to the fish story.) The children are catching a plenitude of fish and all seem to want to eat their catch of the day. Suddenly the prep area is filled with buckets full of water and fish splashing about. Being the one in charge, I issue the order to kill the fish, clean them and put them on the grill. The faces of my loyal staff all now look like deer caught in headlights. It seems no one has actually killed a fish before. The lesson begins. It's all in the wrist and the sturdiness of the tabletop you hit it on. The deed is done, the fish are cooked. The children seem unimpressed that the heads are still on their food and do not completely trust they are about to eat the actual fish they caught. Children are very astute.

I'm not sure what event happened next —it's all a bit of a blur from this point on. In the background I hear voices that sound remarkably like Minnie Mouse. Apparently there were some leaking balloons and my very conscientious staff threw their mouths over the leaks in an effort to save the helium from being lost. That's the story they told me and who am I to question them?

The magical Alberta skies have now transformed from glorious blue to angry black and the temperature has dropped about 20 degrees. We are not happy! The skies open up and the rain begins to fall. Harder now, and the tents that are protecting the barbecues from the elements begin to sag a bit with the weight of the water catching on the top. The guests are mostly ranchers and easy-going people, not terribly affected by adverse weather—the party continues. "Put the ribs on," I say, beautiful baby back ribs; we can hardly wait. My assistant comes to me and says, "You better

come look at this." Like a fool, I do. The ribs are now a huge blaze of fire and people are backing away from me. Not to worry, the hail has arrived, the tents can no longer hold back the deluge and the seams begin to leak. All of the seams. We, my trusted assistant and I, are not deterred. We start to cook the steaks. Five or six very important Albertans are now standing in the hail and rain, holding umbrellas over the steaks to keep them dry. (That's right, over the steaks, not us. What would be the point of covering us?)

I should have mentioned that the barbecues and, in fact, the entire cooking/prep area were set up at the bottom of a hill and the ground is now covered in a foot of ice water. We are no longer concerned that the fork lightning is getting very close and people are looking for a safe place to ride out the storm. We continue to cook. That's our job. We are growing weary and the waves kicked up by the high winds are now lapping at our kneecaps. We feel like we are in the Stephen King version of the movie *A River Runs Through It.*

"Steaks are done," we shout. "Great, let's eat," is the response we hear. Like nothing has happened. To the untrained eye, of course, nothing has happened. We are professionals and we were there to do a job. And we did.

We are now on our twenty-first hour of non-stop work for this day. Everything is packed up and a good portion of the staff have headed out, thankful to be alive. The hostess of the party comes to me with praise of how terrific everything was and how she can't believe it came off without a hitch. "Can you stay for a drink?" she asks.

I quickly source out a designated driver, change out of my chef's clothes and sit down for a relaxing beverage. I promptly fall asleep, sitting up without so much as a sip of my long-awaited beverage. My trusted assistant wakes me and we head out on our one-hour drive back to the city.

Now, it is important to remember, I am a trained professional, and this should not be attempted without the supervision of a trained professional. Oh and by the way, every word of this is true.

JUDY WOOD

My "Not-Quite-Disaster" Tale

The bride called at noon.

She wasn't concerned about the groom getting to the church on time. No, the bride had more pressing things on her mind. She wanted to know when the caterer would arrive.

"Umm, we should be there by about two tomorrow afternoon," I said helpfully. "The ceremony is at four, so two hours should be about perfect for set-up."

Dead silence.

Then her voice sounded in my ear, suddenly distant, as if she were half the world removed from me. "Dee," she said, icy calm, "the wedding is today."

It was my turn to be silent. But only for half a minute. "Right," I said. "We'll be there inside the hour."

I flew around the office, throwing papers into my briefcase. Then into the kitchen.

The duck lay in its marinade, taking on character. I tucked the phone under my ear as I threw the duck into the food processor and whirled it into a smooth purée, simultaneously talking to the staff booked for the wedding. "Yes, that's right. Today, not tomorrow. Meet me there and hurry!" On to the cheeses, tumbling them into a plastic tub, then the greens, the skewered meats. I ransacked the shelves filled with labelled sauces and dressings. The toolbox, always loaded and ready, was slung into the van, followed by the ice, the checked list of platters, the waiting bag of linen for the kitchen staff.

A silent string of prayers ran through my head as my feet clattered on the kitchen tiles. Whew! Thank goodness it's all prepped. Thank goodness I write endless lists. Thank goodness the rentals are already on-site, delivered today, in anticipation of a quiet Sunday tomorrow for the rental company. Odd quirk of luck, that.

By now, my brain was running in overdrive, working down the list posted on the board, not even trying to solve how this could have happened. All that mattered was making it work.

We wheeled the van into the driveway, rolled out the trolley, double-timed the stairs. In no time, the duck was rushing through its allotted oven time. Today was not the day for standard techniques, but for flat-out, dead-fast cook-it-on-the-fly *cuisine rapide*.

In the end, after the bride and groom had walked down the aisle, the festive meal was waiting. The caterer and her staff were breathing hard but not discernibly rushing. The entire menu was ready, on time and as requested, for the assembled guests. And only the bride and I knew just how close a brush with disaster had been averted.

It only happened once, and once was too much. But the lesson changed how I did business, adding a layer of confirmation and cross-checking to an already deep layer of paper and planning.

The bride called the next day. "Good timing," she said, laughing.

DEE HOBSBAWN-SMITH

Prawn & Scallop Salad with Tarragon Dressing (p. 89)

Chestnut Ravioli in Roasted Pumpkin Broth (p. 80)

Rosemary Pancetta Pork (p. 128), My Favourite Asparagus Salad (p. 92)
and Roasted Tomato-Stuffed Peppers (p. 180)

Haricot Vert Salad with Figs & Walnut Vinaigrette (p. 88)

MAIN DISHES

ENTRÉES

Shelley WELLY with FOIE GRAS Hollandaise

I suppose I'm guilty, as I'm often charged, of not leaving well enough alone. This can be a good thing. Here the classic preparation of Beef Wellington has the addition of fresh arugula and is finished with a to-die-for foie gras hollandaise sauce. The crispy onions are a fun garnish, and worth the work.

Shelley Robinson

Serves 4 to 6

3 Tbsp.	butter	45 mL
3 Tbsp.	olive oil	45 mL
1	medium onion, finely chopped	1
1 lb.	assorted fresh mushrooms (shiitake, portobello, oyster, chanterelle, morel, whatever is in season), cleaned and coarsely chopped	450 g
2 Tbsp.	finely chopped garlic	30 mL
	salt and freshly ground black pepper to taste	
1 lb.	arugula, washed and roughly chopped	450 g
2 Tbsp.	canola oil	30 mL
3 lbs.	beef tenderloin, centre cut, trimmed of silverskin	1.35 kg
2 lbs.	puff pastry (see Quick Puff Pastry, page 211)	900 g
3 Tbsp.	grainy Dijon mustard	45 mL
3 Tbsp.	foie gras	45 mL
3 Tbsp.	butter	45 mL
2	egg yolks	2
2 tsp.	white wine vinegar	10 mL
3 cups	canola oil	720 mL
1 cup	all-purpose flour	240 mL
1 tsp.	cayenne pepper	5 mL
1 tsp.	white pepper	5 mL
1 cup	finely sliced onions	240 mL

RECOMMENDED WINE: hearty Gigondas from the Rhône or other similar wine from Southern France

Puff Pastry

Puff pastry is difficult, although not impossible, to make from scratch. I recommend checking with your local pâtisserie to see if you might buy some from them. Often, if they make it they will sell it. The frozen supermarket brands puff work well but don't have much flavour. Be sure to always roll the dough cold and bake it cold for the best puff baking.

Shelley Robinson

Preheat a pan large enough to hold the mushrooms and arugula over medium-high heat. Add the 3 Tbsp. (45 mL) butter and olive oil and sauté the onion for 2 to 3 minutes. Add the mushrooms, stirring to coat them in the oil, then add the garlic. Continue to cook and stir until the mushrooms are wilted and all the liquid has evaporated from the pan. Season the mixture well with salt and pepper and stir in the chopped arugula, cooking until it just begins to wilt. Remove from the heat and pour onto a baking sheet to cool.

Preheat a large sauté pan over high heat and add the 2 Tbsp. (30 mL) canola oil. Season the tenderloin with pepper and sear it on all sides, including the ends. Set aside.

Divide the puff pastry into 2 equal pieces. Roll each piece into a rectangle about 3 inches (7.5 cm) larger than the piece of tenderloin. Place one piece of the rolled puff pastry onto a baking sheet, centre the beef on the pastry and spread the top and sides with the mustard. Press the mushroom filling onto the mustard. Brush the exposed pastry border with water and drape the second pastry sheet over top of the beef. Press firmly down on the edges to seal the borders. Cut two small round vents in the top. Brush the cut-out pieces with water and press them on the outside of the pastry as decoration. Place in the freezer for 10 minutes prior to baking.

To cook the beef, preheat the oven to 450°F (230°C). Bake for 15 minutes, then reduce the heat to 350°F (175°C). Bake for another 20 minutes for rare, 30 minutes for medium-rare.

Meanwhile, make the sauce. Combine the foie gras and 3 Tbsp. (45 mL) butter in a food processor until smooth. Remove and refrigerate until cold. Place the egg yolks and vinegar in a stainless steel bowl and whisk over hot water in a double boiler until the mixture is fluffy and thick. Remove from the heat and whisk in the cold foie gras-butter mixture a little at a time. Season with salt and pepper, cover and set aside in a warm but not hot location until ready to serve.

To make the onions, heat the 3 cups (720 mL) canola oil in a large heavy pot or deep fryer to 350°F (175°C). Combine the flour, cayenne pepper and white pepper and toss the onions in the mixture. Working in batches, fry the onions until golden brown and crispy. Drain on paper towels.

When the beef has reached the desired doneness, remove from the oven and allow to rest for at least 5 minutes before slicing. Serve 1 thick slice per person and garnish with the onions.

Beef Short Ribs with Sun-Dried Cherries, Star Anise & Cinnamon

This is an all-time favourite dish for entertaining. The ribs can be made days ahead and reheated, or you can start them in the morning and by the time you arrive home from skiing or hiking the ribs are melt-in-your-mouth ready and the house is filled with a spicy aroma. I serve them with boiled potatoes and parsnips that have been mashed together with lots of butter and cream.

RECOMMENDED WINE:
Argentinian malbec or inexpensive Spanish tempranillo

SHELLEY ROBINSON

SERVES 6

12	3-inch (7.5-cm) beef short ribs, each tied tightly around the middle with butcher twine	12
2 Tbsp.	freshly ground cinnamon	30 mL
2 Tbsp.	freshly ground whole star anise	30 mL
2 Tbsp.	kosher salt	30 mL
1 Tbsp.	freshly ground black pepper	15 mL
4	large shallots, thinly sliced	4
6	cloves garlic	6
6 cups	dark spicy beer	1.5 L
6 cups	beef stock	1.5 L
1½ cups	sun-dried cherries	360 mL
1	whole cinnamon stick	1
2	whole star anise	2

UNUSUAL MEAT CUTS

Many of the best cuts of meat are not sold in those little styrofoam containers, so you need to get to know a butcher or two to help you get the good stuff. Often anything that is not a regular item will have to be preordered and may arrive frozen, so give them lots of warning. And I've found it doesn't hurt to butter them up a bit by letting them know how much you truly appreciate their specialized service and product. Butchers are a proud bunch and, sadly, a fading breed.

SHELLEY ROBINSON

Preheat the oven to 375°F (190°C). Place the ribs in a roasting pan that is large enough to hold all the liquid that will be added. Combine the ground cinnamon and star anise, salt and pepper, and season the ribs with the mixture, coating all sides with the spices. Scatter the shallots and garlic in and around the ribs. Place in the oven and roast, turning occasionally, for 30 to 45 minutes, until all sides are golden brown. Pour the beer and stock over the ribs and return to the oven for about 20 minutes, or until the liquid begins to boil.

Reduce the heat in the oven to 275°F (135°C). Scatter the cherries, cinnamon stick and whole star anise over the ribs and cover with a lid or foil. Depending on the size of the vessel, you may or may not need to turn the ribs during the cooking time. If the ribs are completely covered or 90% covered in liquid, there is no need to turn them. If the ribs are less than 90% covered in liquid you will want to turn them at least once halfway through the cooking process. The ribs should cook for a minimum of 3 hours, but up to 5 hours is ideal. After this long cooking the ribs will indeed be falling off the bone. Remove them from the braising liquid carefully with tongs and place in another baking dish. Cover and keep warm as you prepare the sauce.

The liquid will be quite "fatty" from the ribs, so carefully pour the liquid into a taller saucepan and skim off the fat floating on the top using a ladle or large spoon. When all the fat has been skimmed off, turn the heat to high and reduce the sauce until it begins to have a slightly syrupy consistency, about 20 minutes. Remove the string from the ribs and serve with the sauce spooned over each one.

Succulent Beef Curry

This luscious meat curry has intense, incredible flavours. And, yes, that really is 20 cloves of garlic. Serve it with saffron rice pilaf or coconut rice.

Gail Norton

RECOMMENDED BEER:
full-bodied Indian dark beer

Serves 8

½ cup	vegetable oil	120 mL
3	large onions, diced	3
20	cloves garlic, minced	20
1	2-inch (5-cm) piece fresh ginger, grated	1
2 Tbsp.	turmeric	30 mL
3 Tbsp.	water	45 mL
2 Tbsp.	paprika	30 mL
½ cup	tomato paste	120 mL
5 lbs.	stewing beef, cut into cubes	2.25 kg
⅓ cup	ground coriander	80 mL
¼ cup	ground cumin	60 mL
1 Tbsp.	salt	15 mL
2–3 cups	water or beef stock	480–720 mL
1 Tbsp.	hot pepper flakes, or to taste	15 mL
¼ cup	garam masala	60 mL
	minced fresh coriander, for garnish	

Heat the oil in a large pan over medium-high heat. Add the onion, garlic and ginger and sauté until the mixture is golden. Add the turmeric and continue cooking for about 5 minutes. Add the 3 Tbsp. (45 mL) water, then stir in the paprika, tomato paste, beef, coriander, cumin and salt. Cook and stir the mixture over moderate heat for about 10 minutes, or until the beef juices have evaporated. Add the 2–3 cups (480–720 mL) water or beef stock and the hot pepper flakes. Simmer the mixture uncovered, stirring occasionally, for 45 minutes to 1 hour, or until the beef is very tender. Add the garam masala and cook for about 5 minutes more. Garnish the curry with fresh coriander.

Herb Roasted Rack of Veal with Caramelized Apples

Brandy, apples, veal—with these ingredients, need I add more?

SERVES 6

JUDY WOOD

RECOMMENDED WINE: this celebration dinner calls for a fine French red Burgundy!

COOKING MEAT

The best way to determine whether a large cut of meat is perfectly cooked is by using a good quality instant read thermometer. I have a wonderful new model, an electronic thermometer, that takes all the guess work out of cooking a tenderloin like this. All you need to know is the internal temperature. For a rare or medium rare roast (the perfect way to serve this tenderloin), cook to an internal temperature of 140°F-145°F (60°C-63°C). For a medium or well-done beef, cook to 160°F-170°F (70°C-75°C)

5 Tbsp.	olive oil	75 mL
5-lb.	rack of veal, frenched	2.25-kg
½ cup	coarsely chopped mixed fresh thyme, sage and parsley	120 mL
2	cloves garlic, minced	2
1 tsp.	salt	5 mL
1 tsp.	freshly cracked black pepper	5 mL
4 Tbsp.	butter	60 mL
4	large apples, peeled, cored and cut into wedges	4
1 tsp.	sugar	5 mL
½ cup	chopped shallots	120 mL
⅓ cup	brandy	80 mL
1 cup	chicken or veal stock	240 mL
	salt and freshly ground black pepper to taste	

Preheat the oven to 350°F (175°C).

Heat 2 Tbsp. (30 mL) of the oil in a roasting pan on the stovetop over medium heat. Add the veal to the pan and brown on all sides, about 15 to 20 minutes.

In a small bowl combine the mixed fresh herbs, garlic, salt, pepper and remaining 3 Tbsp. (45 mL) olive oil. Rub the fresh herb mixture over the veal. Place in the oven and roast for 1 hour, or until a meat thermometer reads 125°F (52°C). Transfer to a platter and cover with foil while you prepare the apples.

Melt 2 Tbsp. (30 mL) of the butter in the roasting pan. Add the apples and sugar; sauté until the apples are tender and a deep golden brown, about 5 minutes. Add the shallots and sauté for 2 minutes. Add the brandy and boil until it is reduced to a glaze, about 2 minutes, scraping up any brown bits. Add the stock and bring to a boil. Cook until the sauce thickens and is reduced to about half the volume. Season with salt and pepper.

To serve, slice the veal and spoon the apples and sauce over top.

Peppered BEEF FILLET with RED Wine & SHALLOT Sauce

A whole piece of beef tenderloin is expensive but it's one of the easiest ways to impress guests. Make your favourite mashed or roasted potato recipe and steam some colourful vegetables to serve alongside.

RECOMMENDED WINE: Argentinian malbec, Spanish Rioja or French Languedoc blend

CINDA CHAVICH

SERVES 4 TO 6

1	2-lb. (1-kg) piece beef tenderloin, trimmed	1
½ tsp.	salt	2.5 mL
3 Tbsp.	whole black peppercorns, coarsely crushed	45 mL
3 Tbsp.	olive oil	45 mL
1 recipe	Red Wine & Shallot Sauce	1 recipe

Preheat the oven to 400°F (200°C). Bring the tenderloin to room temperature. Sprinkle the meat with salt and roll it in crushed black peppercorns, pressing to coat all sides.

Heat the oil in a roasting pan over medium-high heat and quickly sear the beef on all sides to seal in the juices. Place the pan in the oven and roast until the tenderloin is medium-rare, about 20 to 25 minutes.

Remove the beef to a cutting board and tent with foil. Allow the meat to rest for 10 to 15 minutes before carving into ½-inch (1.2-cm) slices, slightly on the diagonal. Serve 2 to 3 slices per person, drizzled with shallot sauce. Pass the remaining beef and sauce separately.

Red Wine and Shallot Sauce

Makes 2¹⁄₂ cups (600 mL)

2 Tbsp.	butter	30 mL
2 cups	sliced shallots	480 mL
1 tsp.	brown sugar	5 mL
1 Tbsp.	top-quality balsamic vinegar (balsamico tradizionale)	15 mL
1 Tbsp.	minced garlic	15 mL
¹⁄₂ tsp.	dried thyme	2.5 mL
2 cups	beef broth	480 mL
1¹⁄₂ cups	dry red wine	360 mL
¹⁄₄ cup	brandy	60 mL
2 Tbsp.	cornstarch, mixed with 1 Tbsp. (15 mL) water	30 mL

Heat the butter in a sauté pan over medium heat and add the sliced shallots. Sauté until soft and beginning to caramelize, about 15 to 20 minutes. Stir in the sugar, vinegar, garlic and thyme and cook for 5 minutes longer.

Add the beef broth, red wine and brandy. Bring to a boil and simmer until the sauce is reduced to about 2 cups (480 mL), about 30 minutes. Whisk in the cornstarch solution and boil until the sauce is smooth and thick. Set the sauce aside.

Bring the sauce to a boil before serving, whisking in any juices that have accumulated in the roasting pan.

Pot-Roasted BEEF with FLUFFY KASHA PILAF

An eastern European staple, buckwheat groats, or kasha, have a unique smoky flavour that I find addictive. This is a traditional recipe—the method of sautéing the grain quickly with an egg keeps the unique conical kernels separate and fluffy. It's perfect with the gravy that's created when you make this classic pot roast, the best way to end a winter day outdoors.

RECOMMENDED WINE: Cru Bourgeois from Bordeaux or a fruity cabernet franc or malbec

Cinda Chavich

Serves 4 to 6

½ cup	flour	120 mL
½ tsp.	salt	2.5 mL
½ tsp.	freshly ground black pepper	2.5 mL
1	2-lb. (900-g) piece beef brisket or inside round roast	1
¼ cup	canola oil	60 mL
3	large carrots, cut in thick chunks	3
2	large parsnips, cut in chunks	2
1	large onion, chopped	1
2	stalks celery, chopped	2
1	small rutabaga, cubed	1
2 cups	beef broth	480 mL
2 Tbsp.	flour	30 mL
1 Tbsp.	soft butter	15 mL
1 recipe	Fluffy Kasha Pilaf	1 recipe

Preheat the oven to 275° (135°C). Combine the flour, salt and pepper and coat the meat heavily on all sides.

Heat the oil in a Dutch oven over medium-high heat and brown the roast well on all sides, turning it frequently. The meat should be dark brown and evenly crusted. Remove the meat from the pan and set aside.

Add the carrot, parsnip, onion, celery and rutabaga to the hot oil and sauté until tender and beginning to caramelize, about 10 minutes. Set the browned beef on top of the vegetables, pour the broth over top and tightly cover the pan (a layer of foil beneath the lid gives the necessary seal).

Place the covered pan in the oven and cook until the roast is very tender, about 3 to 4 hours. Remove the beef from the pan, place on a warm platter and cover with foil to keep warm.

Skim the excess fat from the cooking liquid. Make a roux by mixing the flour and butter and whisk into the liquid. Bring the gravy back to a boil and cook until it is thick. (Alternately, eliminate the roux and purée the vegetables and cooking liquid to make a sauce.) Slice the beef and serve with the pan gravy, vegetables and kasha.

FLUFFY KASHA PILAF

SERVES 4 TO 6

1 cup	toasted buckwheat groats (kasha)	240 mL
1	egg, lightly beaten	1
1 Tbsp.	olive oil	15 mL
3 Tbsp.	butter	45 mL
1	medium onion, finely chopped	1
2 cups	chicken or vegetable stock	480 mL
$\frac{1}{4}$ tsp.	salt	1.2 mL
2 cups	chopped mushrooms	480 mL
2 tsp.	chopped fresh dill	10 mL

Combine the buckwheat groats and egg in a bowl, stirring to coat the grains well. Set aside.

Heat the olive oil and 1 Tbsp. (15 mL) of the butter in a saucepan with a tight-fitting lid over medium-high heat. Add the onion and cook until soft, about 5 minutes. Add the buckwheat and stir-fry quickly, until the egg is cooked and the grains are separated.

Add the stock and salt and bring to a boil. Cover the pan, reduce the heat to low and simmer for 15 minutes.

Meanwhile, heat the remaining 2 Tbsp. (30 mL) butter in a non-stick pan over medium-high heat. Add the mushrooms and fry until they release their liquid and begin to brown. When the kasha is cooked, fluff it with a fork and stir in the fried mushrooms and dill.

Lamb in a Silky Spinach Curry

The longer you cook the spinach the more succulent it becomes—the spices and spinach meld into one. You can replace the lamb with beef or compressed tofu. I have also used just the spinach mixture as a side dish.

RECOMMENDED WINE:
Australian shiraz or
French syrah blend

GAIL NORTON

SERVES 6 TO 8

2	medium onions, roughly chopped	2
1	2-inch (5-cm) piece fresh ginger, roughly chopped	1
10	cloves garlic	10
2	green chilies	2
½ cup	oil	120 mL
1	cinnamon stick	1
7	cloves	7
7	cardamom pods	7
4	bay leaves	4
2 Tbsp.	ground coriander	30 mL
1 Tbsp.	ground cumin	15 mL
2 tsp.	turmeric	10 mL
2	10½-oz. (300-g) package frozen chopped spinach, thawed	2
2.2 lbs.	stewing beef or lamb	1 kg
	salt to taste	
1 Tbsp.	garam masala	15 mL

Blend the onion, ginger, garlic and chilies in a blender with just enough water to make a smooth purée.

Heat the oil in a large pan over medium-high heat and add the cinnamon stick, cloves, cardamom and bay leaves; cook until the bay leaves turn brown. Carefully add the onion paste, taking care to avoid any splatter. Cook for 10 minutes until the mixture is brown.

Cook and stir over medium heat, adding the coriander, cumin and turmeric and making sure to incorporate each one completely before adding the next. Add the spinach and the beef or lamb, along with the salt. Cover the pan, reduce the heat and let the mixture simmer for about 45 minutes to 1 hour.

Add the garam masala and cook for 2 minutes longer. Don't over-indulge with the garam masala, as it will give the mixture an unpleasant grainy texture.

Note: If you want the spinach mixture to be very silky, purée it after all the spices and spinach have been added, then add the beef or lamb and cook for the remaining hour.

Rack of Lamb
with Balsamic Demi

This is quite enjoyable as a main course but I also like to serve it as an appetizer—many people find lamb a bit rich and only eat it in small amounts. For me, any time is a good time to eat lamb.

RECOMMENDED WINE: rich, complex cabernet or merlot from California or the Pacific Northwest

Judy Wood

Serves 6

2 Tbsp.	vegetable oil	30 mL
2	racks of lamb	2
1/2 tsp.	salt	2.5 mL
1/2 tsp.	pepper	2.5 mL
1/2 cup	balsamic vinegar	120 mL
1 cup	beef or lamb stock	240 mL

Preheat the oven to 425°F (220°C).

Heat the vegetable oil in an ovenproof sauté pan over high heat. Season the racks of lamb with the salt and pepper, then sear them, meaty side down, for 3 minutes. Flip the meat over and sear for another minute. Place the pan in the oven and roast the lamb for about 10 minutes.

Remove the lamb from the pan and cover with foil. Place the pan on the stovetop over high heat and add the balsamic vinegar. Bring to a boil and reduce to about 1 Tbsp. (15 mL). Add the stock and boil until it is reduced to 1/2 cup (120 mL).

To serve, slice the rack into individual servings and coat well with the sauce.

Lamb BURGER with Cambozola and CARAMELIZED Onions

RECOMMENDED WINE:
Portuguese red from the
Douro, or a grenache/
syrah blend from the
Languedoc

These three strong flavours come together beautifully. This is not for everyone, but you may be pleasantly surprised if you give it a chance.

SERVES 6

JUDY WOOD

1 Tbsp.	butter	15 mL
3	shallots, minced	3
1 lb.	ground lamb	450 g
3 Tbsp.	dry bread crumbs	45 mL
1	egg	1
2 Tbsp.	Worcestershire sauce	30 mL
1 tsp.	Dijon mustard	5 mL
3 Tbsp.	butter	45 mL
1	large onion, sliced	1
1 Tbsp.	sugar	15 mL
1	portobello mushroom (optional)	1
6	freshly baked buns	6
6 oz.	Cambozola cheese	170 g

Preheat the grill. Melt the butter in a small pan over medium heat. Add the shallots and sauté for 3 minutes. Remove from the heat and let cool.

In a bowl combine the shallots, lamb, bread crumbs, egg, Worcestershire sauce and Dijon. Stir well. Divide the mixture into 6 equal portions then shape into thick patties. Grill over medium heat for 5 minutes on each side for medium-rare, or until done to your liking.

Melt the butter in a frying pan over medium heat. Add the sliced onion and sugar and cook for about 10 minutes, until the onion is brown and is reduced to half the volume.

Slice the portobello mushroom, if using, and grill over medium-high heat for 2 minutes on each side.

Slice the buns and place each on a serving plate. Build the burger by placing the Cambozola on top of the hot burger so it has an opportunity to melt. Add the onions and mushroom slices and enjoy.

Stuffed Glazed Loin Chops on a Bed of Warmed Lentils

My fellow "Dishing" cooks gave me no amount of teasing about my fondness for walnuts—they seemed to be in almost everything I suggested for inclusion in the new book. This was one that they allowed and I got walnuts in many ways into this one (they all loved the outcome, so never mind the snide comments).

RECOMMENDED WINE:
Australian semillon blend or similar from California or the Pacific Northwest

GAIL NORTON

SERVES 6

For the pork chops:

3 oz.	dried wild mushroom mix	85 mL
2 cups	sherry	480 mL
2 Tbsp.	butter	30 mL
1/4 cup	olive oil	60 mL
2 cups	fresh cultivated mushrooms, sliced	480 mL
4	shallots, finely chopped	4
2/3 cup	cracker crumbs	160 mL
1 tsp.	coarsely crushed black pepper	5 mL
1/2 cup	grated hard Fontina cheese	120 mL
2/3 cup	walnuts, lightly toasted	160 mL
2 tsp.	kosher salt	10 mL
4 Tbsp. + 6 Tbsp.	walnut oil	60 mL + 90 mL
6	pork loin chops, cut at least 1 inch (2.5 cm) thick	6
1/2 cup	olive oil	120 mL
2/3 cup	finely cut Seville orange marmalade	160 mL

Soak the mushroom mix for at least 1 hour in the sherry. Melt the butter with the 1/4 cup (60 mL) olive oil over medium heat, making sure the butter does not begin to brown. Add the cultivated mushrooms and shallots and sauté until the mixture begins to soften and becomes fragrant, about 10 minutes.

Squeeze out the reconstituted wild mushrooms to remove most of the liquid, reserving the soaking liquid. Coarsely chop the mushrooms and add to the sautéed mixture. Cook for another 10 minutes. Remove from the heat and add the crumbs, pepper, cheese, walnuts, salt and 4 Tbsp. (60 mL) walnut oil.

Preheat the oven to 350°F (175°C). Create a cavity in each pork chop by using a paring knife to cut a small incision and enlarging it on the inside. (As an alternative, have your butcher butterfly the chop, stuff and close it with a skewer.) Stuff each chop to capacity with the mushroom mixture and use a skewer to hold it closed.

SEL MARIN DE BRETAGNE

The search for new and interesting salts brings Sel Marin de Bretagne to our salt bowl. It has been hand-gathered and sun-dried; the salt is in small chunks and its grey colour is because it retains some residual minerals from the salt beds where it is gathered. You will find it to be more intensely "salty" than kosher salt or fleur de sel, with a pleasant aftertaste because of the minerals. Sel Marin de Bretagne can be used in your regular cooking but it shines as a finishing garnish to such summer delights as ripe red tomatoes.

GAIL NORTON

Heat the ½ cup (120 mL) olive oil in a large frying pan over high heat. Add the chops and brown on both sides. Place in a baking dish large enough to hold the chops in a single layer.

Combine the marmalade and 6 Tbsp. (90 mL) of walnut oil and spread half on the chops. Place in the oven and bake the chops until firm, about 30 minutes

Heat the olive oil in a large saucepan over medium heat. Add the sausage and cook until brown. Remove the sausage and set aside. Add the onion, garlic and red pepper to the pan and sauté until slightly soft. Add the lentils, green onion and parsley and stir to coat. Add the stock and gently simmer, covered, until the lentils are soft but not mushy, about 25 to 40 minutes. Do not let the mixture become dry; add more stock or water as required.

For the lentils:

6 Tbsp.	olive oil	90 mL
1 lb.	smoked sausage, sliced	450 g
2	small onions, chopped	2
8	cloves garlic, minced	8
2	red bell peppers, chopped	2
2 cups	green lentils, preferably du Puy lentils	480 mL
2	bunches green onions, sliced	2
½ cup	fresh parsley	120 mL
8 cups	chicken stock	2 L
½ cup	corn kernels	120 mL
½ cup	red wine vinegar	120 mL
½ cup	walnut oil	120 mL
2 tsp.	salt	10 mL
2 tsp.	freshly ground black pepper	10 mL

Slice the reserved sausage into chunks and add to the lentils. Add the corn, vinegar and walnut oil and simmer with the lid off. Cook until the liquids are reduced and it is a stew-like consistency, about 20 minutes. Season with salt and pepper.

To serve heat the remaining marmalade glaze and top the chops. Spread about 3⁄4 cup (180 mL) of the warm lentil salad on each plate, keeping it to one side. Top with the glazed, stuffed chop.

Grilled Lamb Chops with Molasses Glaze & Tomato Prosciutto Sauce

For years the only way I ever tasted lamb was drenched in mint sauce and that was only on rare occasions. Now I love the taste of lamb but find I still only prepare it for special meals. The tomato prosciutto sauce makes an unusual but delicious addition.

RECOMMENDED WINE: bold Italian Barbaresco or Spanish Rioja

RHONDDA SIEBENS

SERVES 4

1	prosciutto hock	1
1	yellow onion, peeled and halved	1
2	carrots, peeled	2
4	stalks celery	4
2	cloves garlic	2
4	black peppercorns	4
1	bay leaf	1
1	28-oz. (796-mL) can stewed tomatoes	1
	salt and freshly ground black pepper to taste	
12	rib lamb chops	12
3 Tbsp.	olive oil	45 mL
1 Tbsp.	sea salt	15 mL
1/3 cup	molasses	80 mL
1/3 cup	Madeira	80 mL
2	cloves garlic, peeled and crushed	2
1 1/2 cups	Tomato Prosciutto Sauce	360 mL

Make a stock by combining the prosciutto hock, onion, carrots, celery, garlic, peppercorns and bay leaf in a stockpot. Add water to cover and simmer for approximately 2 hours. Reserve 3/4 cup (180 mL) of the stock.

Take the prosciutto hock from the stock and break the soft parts into smaller pieces. Place in a food processor and process with some of the stock to make a coarse purée. Add the tomatoes, season with salt and pepper and pulse again. This is your sauce.

Preheat the oven to 350°F (175°C). Place the lamb chops in a shallow dish and coat with the olive oil and sea salt. Preheat a grill to very high and sear the lamb chops on both sides briefly.

Place the molasses, reserved stock, wine and crushed garlic in a saucepan over medium heat and cook until it's reduced to approximately 1/2 cup (120 mL). Place the lamb chops in an oven-proof serving dish and pour the glaze mixture over them, coating them thoroughly. Bake for 15 minutes.

TO SERVE:

Arrange 3 chops on each plate and drizzle generously with the tomato prosciutto sauce.

Tamarind Lamb Curry with Kaffir Lime Leaves

RECOMMENDED WINE:
big, fruity red from
Australia (shiraz), California
cabernet or zinfandel

This is a quick curry, full of colour and spice, perfection on a bed of simple basmati rice or rice noodles. Do not be tempted to use a shoulder or lesser cut of meat unless you are willing to wait for several hours while the meat cooks to tender! Look for kaffir lime leaves and Thai chilies in Asian markets.

Kaffir Lime Leaves

Kaffir lime leaves will permeate your curry, your clothes and your kitchen with the pure and rather intoxicating scent of lime. There is nothing else like it, no substitute, and no replacement. Find whole kaffir lime leaves, fresh or frozen, in good Asian markets. Don't bother buying the dried ones—they never regain that scent of lime.

DEE HOBSBAWN-SMITH

SERVES 4   DEE HOBSBAWN-SMITH

1 Tbsp.	sunflower oil	15 mL
1	onion, sliced	1
4	cloves garlic, minced	4
2	carrots, julienned	2
½	red bell pepper, julienned	½
¼–½ lb.	lamb loin or leg, sliced	113–225 g
1–2 Tbsp.	curry paste	15–30 mL
3	kaffir lime leaves	3
2 Tbsp.	minced fresh cilantro	30 mL
¼ cup	dry white wine	60 mL
2 cups	chicken or veal stock	480 mL
2 cups	sliced green beans	480 mL
6 oz.	coconut milk	180 mL
1 Tbsp.	honey	15 mL
	juice and zest of ½ lemon	
1 Tbsp.	cornstarch dissolved in cold water	15 mL
1–2	Thai chilies, minced (optional)	1–2
	salt and hot chili flakes to taste	
	minced fresh cilantro, for garnish	

Heat the oil in a heavy pot over medium-high heat. Add the onion, garlic, carrots and pepper and fry until the vegetables are tender. Add the lamb and brown in the hot oil. Add the curry paste and kaffir lime leaves, stir well and cook until fragrant. Add the cilantro and wine. Bring to a boil, then add the stock. Simmer until the meat is tender, 5 to 10 minutes, then add the beans and cook, uncovered, until they are tender and bright green. Stir in the coconut milk, then add the honey and lemon zest and juice. Thicken the curry with the cornstarch dissolved in cold water, boiling it briefly to cook the starch. Add the chilies, if desired. Balance the flavours with salt and hot chili flakes. Serve hot, garnished with minced cilantro.

HERB-CRUSTED LAMB CHOPS WITH OLIVE AÏOLI

This recipe is great for entertaining, but fast enough for anytime! Use your food processor to make the herb crust, then the aïoli. The lamb cooks in 15 minutes or less. Vary the herbs in the crust (mint would be nice, too, in place of the basil). Do use an interesting bread for the crumbs, one that you would want to eat on its own.

RECOMMENDED WINE: robust red from Southern France or hearty Rioja from Spain

PAM FORTIER

SERVES 4

2	slices good bread	2
1 Tbsp.	chopped fresh rosemary	15 mL
1 Tbsp.	chopped fresh thyme	15 mL
1 Tbsp.	chopped fresh basil	15 mL
	freshly ground black pepper to taste	
8	lamb chops	8
	olive oil, for drizzling	
2 Tbsp.	olive oil	30 mL
1 recipe	Olive Aïoli	1 recipe

Place the bread in a food processor fitted with the metal blade. Process to make fine crumbs. Add the herbs and pepper and process for a minute or so more. Place on a plate or in a shallow bowl. Drizzle the chops with olive oil and rub with your hands to coat them thoroughly. Dredge the chops, one at a time, in the herb mixture, pressing the crumb mixture to help it adhere. Set aside on a clean plate.

Preheat the oven to 400°F (200°C). Place the 2 Tbsp. (30 mL) olive oil in an ovenproof frying pan and heat over medium-high. Add the chops and fry for a couple of minutes on each side to obtain a nicely browned crust. Place the pan in the oven and bake for 3 to 5 minutes, or until the desired doneness. To serve, place a dollop of aïoli on each chop and pass the rest separately.

Olive Aïoli

Makes about 1$\frac{1}{2}$ cups (360 mL)

3	cloves garlic, minced	3
2	large egg yolks	2
2 Tbsp.	lemon juice	30 mL
1$\frac{1}{4}$ cups	extra virgin olive oil	300 mL
12	kalamata olives, pitted and coarsely chopped	12
	salt and freshly ground pepper to taste	

Place the garlic, egg yolks and lemon juice in the bowl of a food processor fitted with a metal blade. Process to combine. With the machine running, very slowly drizzle the oil into the mixture through the feed tube. The mixture will emulsify, creating a thick, spoonable sauce. Add the olives, process briefly to combine, and season with salt and pepper.

Classic LAMB Shanks

Lamb shanks are one of the best-kept secret bargains of cooking. One shank per person is enough, except for hearty eaters. Have your butcher cut each shank into three sections (each section will be about 3 inches/7.5 cm long), and use the bony narrow end in your stock pot. Use rich brown stock made with veal or beef bones for this dish, although lamb bones and turkey or chicken carcasses, well-browned for depth of colour and flavour, make for a slightly less rich finish. Serve a nutty barley risotto, mashed spuds or simple noodles and a salad with a sharply acidic vinaigrette to offset the rich nature of this dish.

RECOMMENDED WINE: big, bold red, like a syrah blend from California or an Australian shiraz

DEE HOBSBAWN-SMITH   SERVES 6

2 Tbsp.	olive oil	30 mL
2	onions, thickly sliced	2
1	bulb garlic, cloves separated and peeled	1
4	carrots, peeled and roughly chopped	4
2	stalks celery, roughly chopped	2
2	bay leaves	2
3	sprigs fresh rosemary, minced	3
4	sprigs fresh thyme, minced	4
6	lamb shanks, each cut into 3-inch (7.5-cm) pieces	6
$\frac{1}{2}$	bottle robust red wine	$\frac{1}{2}$
4 cups	rich brown stock	950 mL
$\frac{1}{2}$ cup	canned tomato, seeded and chopped	120 mL
	freshly ground black pepper to taste	
	kosher salt to taste	

Preheat the oven to 350°F (175°C).

Heat the oil in a heavy sauté pan over medium heat. Add the onions, garlic, carrots, celery and bay leaves. Brown well, then add the rosemary and thyme. Transfer the browned herbs and vegetables to a brazier or heavy ovenproof casserole. Return the sauté pan to the stove, add a little oil if needed, and add the lamb shanks in a single layer. If necessary, work in two successive batches rather than overcrowd the pan. Brown all the surfaces of the shanks, then lay them in a single layer on top of the vegetables. Tip out and discard any accumulated fat in the pan, then

add the wine to the sauté pan. Bring the wine to a boil and simmer for 5 minutes. Pour over the lamb. Heat the stock in the sauté pan, then pour it over the lamb along with the tomatoes. Crack some pepper over the entire dish and season with salt.

Place a piece of parchment directly onto the surface of the food, then cover it snugly with tinfoil and a lid. Place in the oven on the centre rack and cook for 3 hours. Check the meat, and if it is tender and pulls easily off the bone, remove the casserole from the oven. Reduce the oven temperature to 200°F (95°C).

Transfer the meat to a shallow gratin dish. Strain the braising juices, pushing firmly on the solids with a wooden spoon to extract absolutely everything. Turn the lamb to coat each piece with juice, season with salt and return the lamb to the oven, uncovered. Cook for another 20 to 30 minutes, turning the lamb several times. Serve hot with the remaining juice spooned onto the plates.

Lemon Thyme Pork Loin Roast with Roasted Pears & Squash

This dish is a nice combination of fresh flavours and comfort food—the roasted pears and squash are comforting and the lemon is very refreshing. You can substitute your favourite squash or root vegetable for the butternut squash.

RECOMMENDED WINE: dry, full-bodied Rosé from the Languedoc, or a luscious New World pinot noir

JUDY WOOD

SERVES 6

3-lb.	pork loin roast	1.35-kg
1/3 cup	olive oil	80 mL
	salt and freshly ground black pepper to taste	
5	cloves garlic, crushed	5
1	bunch fresh thyme	1
2	lemons	2
1-lb.	butternut squash	450-g
4	pears (preferably red)	4
1/2 cup	white wine	120 mL
1 cup	chicken or vegetable stock	240 mL

Preheat the oven to 450°F (230°C).

Place the pork loin in a roasting pan or a large ovenproof container. Pour the olive oil over the loin, then add the salt, pepper, garlic and thyme. (Do not chop the thyme—just pull the herbs off the twig by running your fingers along the stem.) With a vegetable peeler, peel off long pieces of the lemon rind and add them to the pan. Cut the lemon in half and squeeze the juice over the pork. Marinate in the refrigerator for at least 1 hour and up to 3 hours.

Place the pork loin in the oven and roast for 20 minutes; it should be browned on the outside. While the roast is browning, peel the squash and cut it into 1 1/2-inch (3.8-cm) pieces. Cut each pear into 4 wedges and remove the cores. Add the squash and pears to the roasting pan, reduce the heat to 350°F (175°C) and continue cooking for 20 to 25 minutes.

Remove everything from the pan and cover with foil to keep warm. Place the pan on the stovetop over medium heat. Add the white wine and cook for about 5 minutes. Make sure that you use a wooden spoon to get all the little bits from the bottom of the pan. Add the stock and cook until it is reduced by about half. Season with salt and pepper. Slice the roast and serve with squash and pears. Serve the jus on the side.

Pork TENDERLOIN Bathed in Espresso, RED Wine & GRAPES

RECOMMENDED WINE:
full-bodied Cru Beaujolais,
or pinot noir from the USA

One night a friend and I tasted the red wine, grape and espresso combination as a dessert. It wasn't sweet, more like a condiment, and we both commented that it would be interesting when paired with some sort of meat. We thought beef would be too heavy and chicken might not hold up to the intense flavours of the sauce. This is the result—quick and stunning! Serve alongside whipped potatoes and a small salad.

SERVES 4   JANET WEBB

2 Tbsp.	olive oil	30 mL
1	shallot, minced	1
4 cups	mixed seedless grapes	950 mL
½ cup	brewed espresso	120 mL
1 cup	dry red wine	240 mL
2	sticks cinnamon, broken in half	2
2 Tbsp.	honey	30 mL
2 Tbsp.	balsamic vinegar	30 mL
2 Tbsp.	unsalted butter	30 mL
2 Tbsp.	olive oil	30 mL
2	pork tenderloins, approximately 1 lb. (450 g), cleaned of sinew	2

Preheat the oven to 350°F (175°C). Heat 2 Tbsp. (30 mL) olive oil in a medium saucepan. Add the shallot and sauté over medium heat until soft and fragrant, 2 to 3 minutes. Add the grapes and sauté for another minute. Add the espresso, red wine, cinnamon sticks and honey. Stir for 2 to 3 minutes and remove from the heat. Add the vinegar and butter to the pan and stir until the butter melts.

Place the remaining 2 Tbsp. (30 mL) olive oil in a sauté pan over high heat. Quickly sear the tenderloins, one at a time, on all sides. Place the meat in a roasting pan and roast for 20 to 30 minutes for medium. Let the meat sit for 5 minutes before slicing on the diagonal. Place on the serving plates. Quickly reheat the sauce and ladle onto or around the meat. Garnish with the cinnamon sticks.

Peasant Cabbage Dinner (Choucroute)

This Victorian-style recipe has been a tradition in the Dibblee family for hundreds of years. Empire Loyalists during the American Revolution who crossed the border into New Brunswick, their version of this dish includes vinegar, which is the secret of its taste. Earthy, wholesome and inexpensive, it is full of flavour and perfect for winter days. Feel free to substitute any cheap cut of pork for the hocks. Serve family-style on a large platter in the centre of the table.

RECOMMENDED WINE: a classic Alsatian dish should have a classic gewurztraminer or pinot gris from the same area

RHONDDA SIEBENS   SERVES 4

3	pork hocks, whole	3
3	bay leaves	3
12	medium potatoes, peeled	12
8	carrots, halved	8
2	onions, quartered	2
1	head green cabbage	1
6 Tbsp.	white vinegar	90 mL
3 Tbsp.	butter	45 mL

Trim the fat off the pork hocks. Place them in a large pot and cover with water. Add the bay leaves and boil for approximately 45 minutes.

Lower the temperature and add the potatoes, then the carrots and then the onions.

Quarter the cabbage, making sure the core is intact. There should be some core on each quarter to hold the piece together. Set the cabbage on top of the other ingredients in the pot (like a hat or roof). Simmer on low for 1 hour.

Serve on a platter. Pour some of the juice over top. Shake or drizzle the vinegar on top and dot with the butter.

SANSHO-PEPPERED TUNA WITH MOCK-GUAC

RECOMMENDED WINE:
Spanish albarino or Italian pinot grigio

"Mock-guac" is short for mock guacamole. Sansho pepper, available in Japanese specialty stores, is the ground-up bark of the prickly ash tree (the Chinese call it Szechuan pepper). It has a lovely flavour reminiscent of lemon, licorice and pepper—once you have it in your pantry you will dream up all sorts of uses for it.

SERVES 4   GAIL NORTON

1 lb.	tuna	450 g
4 tsp.	sansho pepper	20 mL
2 cups	peas	480 mL
1/4 cup	minced cilantro	60 mL
2	cloves garlic, minced	2
2	limes, zest and juice	2
	several pinches sugar	
	salt and freshly ground black pepper to taste	
1/4 cup	fresh corn kernels or canned corn	60 mL
	whole cilantro leaves, for garnish	

Cut the tuna into 4 pieces and sprinkle each piece with 1 tsp. (5 mL) sansho pepper. Set the tuna aside while preparing the guacamole.

Mash together the peas, cilantro, garlic, lime zest and juice, sugar, salt and pepper. Taste, adjust the seasonings and add the corn.

Preheat the barbecue on high. Place the tuna on the grill, reduce the heat to medium and grill for about 8 minutes. Flip and cook on the other side for about 3 minutes. The amount of time will vary according to the thickness of the fish. The tuna should still be slightly pink on the inside. Cooking too long will produce a tough and unappetizing fish.

To serve, put a dollop of the mock-guac in the middle of each plate. Slice the tuna and arrange it in a fan around the guacamole. Garnish with a cilantro leaf.

The Not So Classic BLT

I have a habit of trying to come up with miniature versions of great flavour combos to pass around at cocktail parties. This was a little fussy as a miniature sandwich, but it makes a substantial sandwich that is a meal in itself. Great for casual get-togethers—it has lots of flavour, it's crunchy and it looks good on a platter with the arugula leaves hanging out. The leftover aïoli has a multitude of uses—sauce for steamed new potatoes or a dip for french fries are just two. It will keep for 3 days in the refrigerator.

RECOMMENDED WINE: slightly chilled Cru Beaujolais or fruity sauvignon blanc

KAREN MILLER

SERVES 6

18	thin slices spicy pancetta	18
12	slices sourdough or multi-grain bread	12
½ cup	Homemade Aïoli	120 mL
4	tomatoes, sliced	4
1	bunch arugula leaves, trimmed	1
	salt and freshly ground black pepper to taste	

Preheat the oven to 350°F (175°C). Place the pancetta slices on a baking sheet and bake until crispy, 4 to 8 minutes, depending on the thickness. Place the bread slices on a baking sheet and toast in the oven until lightly browned. Smother with the homemade aïoli or your favourite store-bought mayonnaise. Place the tomato slices over the mayonnaise and top with 3 pancetta slices and the arugula leaves. Season with salt and pepper and cut into triangles.

Homemade Aïoli

MAKES ABOUT 1½ CUPS (360 mL)

2	cloves garlic, minced	2
	sea salt to taste	
2	large egg yolks	2
1 cup	olive oil	240 mL
½ tsp.	lemon juice	2.5 mL
	freshly ground black pepper (optional)	

Mash the garlic with the salt in a large sturdy bowl. Whisk in the egg yolks and continue whisking until the yolk mixture is thick and pale yellow. Gradually whisk in the olive oil, adding very small amounts at a time, until thick and creamy. Season with more salt if necessary and add the lemon juice and black pepper, if desired.

WRAPPED CHICKEN
WITH SAGE & PROSCIUTTO

RECOMMENDED WINE:
pinot grigio from the
Alta Adige in Italy or a
full-bodied Vernaccia

This is so easy it is scary. Fresh sage is quite strong-tasting but
when combined with the juices from the chicken and the strong
flavour of prosciutto, it almost seems mellow. This makes a great
buffet dish; large quantities can be prepared ahead and cooked
in the oven at the last minute. Slicing the breasts before serving
shows off the sage leaves against the creamy white chicken meat
and the crispy browned prosciutto.

SERVES 4   KAREN MILLER

2	whole boneless chicken breasts, skin on, cut in half	2
1	bunch fresh sage leaves	1
3 Tbsp.	Dijon mustard	45 mL
8	slices prosciutto	8
	salt and freshly ground black pepper to taste	

Push the sage leaves under the skin of the chicken breasts. Coat
the chicken breasts with mustard and wrap 2 slices of prosciutto
around each breast. Place on a baking sheet. (The chicken can
be prepared ahead of time to this point and refrigerated for up
to 1 day.)

Preheat the oven to 375°F (190°C). Salt and pepper the chicken
breasts and bake for 25 minutes. Serve the breasts whole or
slice them and fan them over the plate for a more elegant
presentation.

Rosemary Pancetta Pork with Gorgonzola Potato Gratin

This recipe is based on one by Biba Gaggiano, Italian cookbook author and restaurant owner. The combination of rosemary and pancetta (Italian unsmoked bacon) with the pork is sure to become a favourite once you try it. While you are at the Italian market buying pancetta for the pork roast, purchase some Gorgonzola for the gratin. Many people are familiar with Cambozola, which I refer to as Gorgonzola with "training wheels" because the blue is tempered by being sandwiched between two creamy, Brie-type layers of cheese. Gorgonzola is for people who want even more blue cheese flavour than Cambozola offers.

RECOMMENDED WINE:
Italian barbera or Chianti Riserva

Pam Fortier

Serves 6 to 8

¹⁄₂ lb.	spicy pancetta, not too thinly sliced	225 g
2 ¹⁄₂–3-lb.	boneless pork loin roast	1.1–1.35-kg
4	sprigs fresh rosemary	4

Preheat the oven to 350°F (175°C). Cut 5 lengths of kitchen string, each 24 inches (60 cm) long. On a clean countertop or cutting board, lay two of the strings in the centre of the work space and parallel to the edge of the counter, about 2 inches (5 cm) apart. Lay the remaining three strings across these, centring them, again about 2 inches (5 cm) apart. Arrange approximately ¹⁄₃ of the pancetta (overlap the pieces by at least half for a nice thick covering of bacon) over the grid that has been formed in the centre of the strings. Place the pork loin over the pancetta. Place the remaining pancetta over the top, ends and sides of the roast. Bring the strings up and around the roast, one at a time, and tie them to enclose the pancetta and pork loin. If you can find a volunteer to place a finger on the string while you tie the knots it is much easier! Trim the string ends. You should have a relatively neat bundle. Tuck any loose pieces of pancetta under the string. Tuck the rosemary sprigs under the string, one on top and the other two on the long sides. Cut the fourth sprig in half and tuck a piece on either end.

Roast for approximately 1¹⁄₂ hours, or until the internal tempera-ture reaches 140°F (60°C). This will result in pork which is slightly pink. Cook to 150 to 160°F (65 to 70°C) if you like your pork well done. Remove from the oven and let rest for approximately 10 minutes before carving.

Gorgonzola Potato Gratin

3 Tbsp.	unsalted butter	45 mL
2 cups	whole milk	480 mL
1	clove garlic, peeled and lightly crushed	1
½ cup	cubed or crumbled Gorgonzola cheese	120 mL
3 lbs.	potatoes, preferably russet, peeled and thinly sliced	1.5 kg
	salt and freshly ground black pepper to taste	
2¾ cups	whipping cream	660 mL

Preheat the oven to 350°F (175°C). Butter a 9- x 13-inch (23- x 33-cm) baking dish. Place the milk and garlic in a pot and heat just until scalding. Add the Gorgonzola and stir in. Leave this to melt and infuse.

Place half of the potatoes in a layer in the bottom of the prepared baking dish. Season with salt and pepper. Add the remaining potatoes.

Remove the garlic clove from the milk. Add the cream and combine. Pour over the potatoes. Dot with the remaining butter. Season with salt and pepper. Bake for 1 to 1½ hours, or until the potatoes are soft when pierced with a sharp knife.

Pork Tenderloin
with Rhubarb Chutney

I love to cook pork tenderloin for parties—like a chicken breast or steak, it's the perfect cut to cook quickly, just before serving, and it's always lean and tender. This recipe, with its spicy fruit chutney, was inspired by a dish I tried at de Montreuil's restaurant in Kelowna, B.C. Look for bright red, small rhubarb when it's fresh in the spring to give this sauce a lovely pink colour. If it's winter, and you're stuck with unappealing green, frozen rhubarb, consider adding some cranberries to the chutney for vibrant colour.

RECOMMENDED WINE: pretty rosé from Languedoc or Provence or Cru Beaujolais

CINDA CHAVICH

SERVES 6

1 Tbsp.	chopped fresh thyme	15 mL
2 Tbsp.	Dijon mustard	30 mL
1 tsp.	balsamic vinegar	5 mL
2 tsp.	honey	10 mL
	salt and freshly ground black pepper to taste	
2 Tbsp.	olive oil	30 mL
3	pork tenderloins, about 1 lb. (450 g) each	3
1 recipe	Rhubarb Chutney	1 recipe

Combine the thyme, mustard, vinegar, honey, salt and pepper. Rub the meat with this mixture on all sides, then set aside for 15 minutes. Preheat the oven to 400°F (200°C).

Heat the olive oil in a non-stick sauté pan over high heat and sear the pork tenderloins on all sides, for about 2 minutes in total. Place the pan in the oven and roast the meat for 15 to 20 minutes, until the pork is just cooked to medium. It should still be slightly pink and juicy inside. Place the pork on a cutting board, tent with foil and let rest for 5 to 10 minutes.

To serve, carve the pork diagonally into slices and fan on individual plates. Spoon some of the chutney over the meat and pass the rest.

Rhubarb Chutney

Makes 3 cups (720 mL)

3 cups	chopped red rhubarb	720 mL
1/2	red onion, diced	1/2
1	jalapeño pepper, minced	1
2 Tbsp.	minced fresh ginger	30 mL
2	cloves garlic, minced	2
1/4 cup	honey	60 mL
1/4 cup	brown sugar	60 mL
2 Tbsp.	Worcestershire sauce	30 mL
1/2 cup	hard apple cider or natural unfiltered and unsweetened apple juice	120 mL
2 Tbsp.	apple cider vinegar	30 mL
3	Granny Smith apples, peeled, cored and cubed	3
	hot pepper sauce (optional)	

Combine the rhubarb, onion, jalapeño, ginger, garlic, honey, brown sugar, Worcestershire sauce, cider or juice and vinegar in a non-reactive saucepan and bring to a rolling boil. Reduce the heat and simmer for 20 minutes, until much of the liquid has evaporated and the sauce has a thick, jam-like consistency.

Add the cubed apples to the sauce and simmer for about 10 minutes longer, until the apples are tender but still chunky. Remove the chutney from the heat and cool to room temperature. Adjust the seasoning with hot sauce if desired. The chutney can be made in advance and refrigerated, covered, for several days. Bring to room temperature or warm before serving.

SHABU-SHABU WITH A TRIO OF ASIAN DIPS

Think of this as an Asian-style fondue. This communal meal works best with close friends. On the other hand, it is the ideal way to strengthen any friendship! There is nothing like time spent crowded around a table in close proximity with half a dozen other hungry people to create closer bonds. Of course, those of us who hail from large families will already be familiar with the gentle jostling that can accompany a meal of this style. After all the meat and fish has been poached and eaten, distribute bowls, ladle out the broth and drink up.

RECOMMENDED BEER/WINE: Asian beer or German riesling

DEE HOBSBAWN-SMITH   SERVES 4 TO 8

4 cups	chicken stock	1 L
2–3	dried black Chinese mushrooms	2–3
2	whole star anise	2
6	slices fresh ginger	6
6	green onions, sliced	6
8	cloves garlic, sliced	8
2	kaffir lime leaves	2
2 Tbsp.	fish sauce	30 mL
	lime juice to taste	
	soy sauce to taste	
	hot chili paste to taste	
2 Tbsp.	minced fresh cilantro	30 mL
1 lb.	shrimp, peeled and deveined	450 g
½ lb.	pork tenderloin, cleaned and thinly sliced	225 g
½ lb.	beef tenderloin, cleaned and thinly sliced	225 g
½ lb.	boneless skinless chicken breast, thinly sliced	225 g
1 recipe	Mustard Dip	1 recipe
1 recipe	Hoisin Dip (page 134)	1 recipe
1 recipe	Sesame Dip (page 134)	1 recipe

Make the broth by simmering the stock with the mushrooms, star anise, ginger, onions, garlic, kaffir lime, fish sauce, lime juice, soy sauce and chili paste until all is fragrant and flavourful, about 30 minutes. Strain and keep hot. Float the cilantro on the hot broth at the last moment before supper starts.

Arrange the shrimp, pork, beef and chicken on separate clean plates. Put the boiling stock into fondue pots, with forks or skewers at close hand. Set out the dips and allow people to cook and feed themselves.

Mustard Dip

Makes about ¾ cup (180 mL)

½ cup	smooth Dijon mustard	120 mL
2 Tbsp.	sesame oil	30 mL
3 Tbsp.	sweet Japanese rice vinegar	45 mL
	melted honey to taste	
	hot chili paste to taste	
	salt to taste	
	minced fresh cilantro to taste	

Stir together and store in the fridge. This dish keeps for weeks in the refrigerator, although the cilantro will soften and darken after 2 to 3 days. Serve it with pork, lamb, grilled foods, Asian foods, and with any sandwich.

CONTINUED OVER PAGE.....

Hoisin Dip

½ cup	hoisin sauce	120 mL
2–3 Tbsp.	lemon juice	30–45 mL
1 Tbsp.	minced fresh cilantro	15 mL
1 Tbsp.	puréed garlic	15 mL
1 Tbsp.	finely grated fresh ginger	15 mL
½ tsp.	hot chili paste	2.5 mL
¼–½ cup	water	60–120 mL
	soy sauce to taste	

Combine the ingredients and adjust the balance with the soy sauce. Good with potstickers, grilled salmon, broth-style fondue. This dip keeps for weeks in the refrigerator, but remember to add the cilantro just before use to prevent the herb from darkening.

Sesame Dip

MAKES ABOUT 1¼ CUPS (300 ML)

1 cup	mayonnaise	240 mL
4 Tbsp.	toasted ground sesame seeds	60 mL
2 Tbsp.	minced green onions	30 mL
1 Tbsp.	minced fresh cilantro	15 mL
1 Tbsp.	sesame oil	15 mL
½ tsp.	hot chili paste or flakes	2.5 mL
1 tsp.	light soy sauce	5 mL
1	lime, juice and zest	1

Combine all the ingredients and adjust the flavours with additional soy and lime juice if needed. Keep this dip refrigerated for up to 4 days. Good with sushi, broth-style fondue, grilled Asian shrimp, pork.

A MELODY OF BLACK & WHITE BEANS TOPPED WITH GRILLED TUNA

RECOMMENDED WINE: riesling from Germany or Alsace

Ancho chili pepper has a wonderful taste that is reminiscent of dried fruit and tobacco and can almost be described as being sweet. Ancho is available in Mexican specialty stores either ground or whole. The contrast between the two colours of beans in this dish makes it especially attractive.

SERVES 6 TO 8   GAIL NORTON

6	4-oz. (115-g) thick slices tuna	6
1 Tbsp.	ancho chili powder	15 mL
1 cup	raw white beans	240 mL
1 cup	raw black beans	240 mL
1/3 cup	olive oil	80 mL
1 Tbsp.	mango chutney	15 mL
1 Tbsp.	finely minced candied ginger	15 mL
1	yellow bell pepper, roasted and diced (see page 46)	1
1	red bell pepper, roasted and diced (see page 46)	1
1/2 cup	diced cucumber	120 mL
4	green onions, green part only, sliced	4
1	bunch fresh cilantro	1
1	bunch fresh parsley	1
1	orange, juice and zest	1
	salt and freshly ground black pepper to taste	

Sprinkle the tuna with the ancho powder, and allow to sit at room temperature for at least an hour (or in the fridge overnight).

Cook the beans separately until softened. (If you were to cook them together, the black bean "ink" would colour the water and they would become one homogenous, unappetizing grey colour.)

In a large bowl, mix the olive oil, chutney and candied ginger. Add the peppers, cucumber, onion, cilantro, parsley and orange zest and juice. Season with salt and pepper. Toss in the cooked beans. Adjust the moisture of the mixture by adding more orange juice or olive oil.

TO SERVE:

Arrange some salad on each plate and top with the tuna.

Preheat the barbecue on high. Place the tuna on the grill, reduce the heat to medium and grill for about 8 minutes. Flip and cook on the other side for about 3 minutes. The amount of time will vary according to the thickness of the fish. The tuna should still be slightly pink on the inside. Cooking too long will produce a tough and unappetizing fish.

TUNA BURGER WITH CUCUMBER
SAKE RIBBONS & WASABI MAYO

A restaurant kitchen that has prime-cut tuna on the dinner menu will likely have some very pricey trimmings and end bits to deal with, and this recipe lends itself perfectly to using these up. As a home cook I find it hard to justify the cost of fresh tuna to prepare this, but some Asian markets may carry sushi-grade tuna, frozen at a fraction of the cost of fresh. You may also find this at your local fishmonger. Tuna is one of my all-time favourite things to eat. I love its meaty qualities without the heaviness of beef.

RECOMMENDED WINE: New World chardonnay with little or no oak

SHELLEY ROBINSON

SERVES 4

1	long English cucumber	1
¼ cup	rice wine vinegar	60 mL
¼ cup	sake	60 mL
2 Tbsp.	sugar	30 mL
1 Tbsp.	salt	15 mL
2 Tbsp.	wasabi powder	30 mL
¼ cup	mayonnaise	60 mL
1½ lbs.	ahi or yellowfin tuna, skin or gristle removed	675 g
3 Tbsp.	minced shallot	45 mL
¼ cup	Japanese pickled ginger, finely chopped	60 mL
2 Tbsp.	Dijon mustard	30 mL
1	anchovy fillet, finely chopped	1
4–5	dashes hot pepper sauce	4–5
3 Tbsp.	finely chopped cilantro	45 mL
2 Tbsp.	extra virgin olive oil	30 mL
	salt and freshly ground black pepper to taste	
½ cup	canola oil	120 mL
4	fresh buns, split and buttered	4

Using a peeler or mandoline, slice the cucumber in long thin slices. Combine the vinegar, sake, sugar and salt in a medium bowl and stir to dissolve the salt and sugar. Add the cucumber slices to the bowl.

Place the wasabi powder in a small bowl, add a few drops of water and stir to make a paste. Slowly stir in the mayonnaise.

With a food grinder, or chopping by hand, grind or chop the tuna to the consistency of hamburger meat. Place the fish in a bowl and combine with the shallot, ginger, mustard, anchovy, hot pepper sauce, cilantro and olive oil. Season with salt and pepper. Divide the tuna into 4 equal balls and shape each into a patty; don't make them too flat or the burgers will overcook.

Preheat a large skillet with the canola oil to very hot. Add the tuna burgers and sear on each side for about 3 minutes. The tuna burger should be served medium-rare.

Remove the cucumber slices from the marinade and place on the bottom of each bun. Place the burger on top with a dollop of wasabi mayo.

Halibut in a Coconut Sauce

For years I would go to my favourite Indian restaurant, the Curry Pot, which is now closed, and order this dish. I just could not bring myself to order anything else because it was so darned delicious. I was surprised and delighted when I was able to recreate this fond memory at home. Look for the coconut cream powder at stores that specialize in Indian food. It's a great way to thicken sauces as well as flavour them with the nutty compelling taste of coconut.

RECOMMENDED WINE:
fruity malvasia or Canadian pinot gris

GAIL NORTON

SERVES 4

3 Tbsp.	olive oil	45 mL
1	medium onion, finely chopped	1
3	cloves garlic, minced	3
1	medium tomato, chopped	1
1	1-inch (2.5-cm) piece fresh ginger	1
2 Tbsp.	hot pepper flakes	30 mL
1 Tbsp.	salt	15 mL
1 Tbsp.	ground cumin	15 mL
1 Tbsp.	ground coriander	15 mL
1 Tbsp.	turmeric	15 mL
3½ oz.	coconut cream powder	100 g
½ cup	water	120 mL
4	pieces halibut	4
1 cup	yogurt or whipping cream	240 mL

Heat the oil in a frying pan over medium-high heat. Sauté the onion and garlic until they are softened and semi-transparent, about 15 minutes. Add the tomato, ginger, hot pepper flakes, salt, cumin, coriander and turmeric. Cook for about 10 minutes.

Mix the coconut cream powder with the water and add it to the pan. Add more water if needed to thin the sauce. Add the halibut pieces and cook until flaky, about 15 minutes. Add the yogurt or whipping cream and cook for about 5 minutes. (If using yogurt, be sure the mixture does not come to a boil, as the sauce will curdle.) Serve immediately.

Asian-Spiced Salmon
with Braised Bok Choy

RECOMMENDED WINE:
California viognier, pinot gris from Alsace or a dry malvasia

Any dry rub or spice mixture, like the five-spice powder, is a shortcut to intense, complex flavours. Chinese five-spice powder has a slight licorice flavour and contains equal amounts of each of ground star anise, Szechuan peppercorns, cinnamon, cloves and fennel seed.

SERVES 4 TO 6   GAIL NORTON

4	salmon fillets	4
2 Tbsp.	Chinese five-spice powder	30 mL
	olive oil	
4	cloves garlic, chopped	4
1	1-inch (2.5-cm) piece fresh ginger, minced	1
1 cup	chicken stock	240 mL
1 Tbsp.	white miso	15 mL
2	medium bok choy, roughly chopped	2

Heat the oven to 400°F (200°C) degrees. Put the salmon fillets on a cookie sheet and sprinkle the Chinese five-spice powder over them. Let the fillets sit for 30 minutes at room temperature. Place in the oven and bake to desired doneness. I prefer to cook salmon for 7 to 8 minutes per inch (2.5 cm), which leaves the salmon moist, with a little line of pink on the inside.

Add enough olive oil to a sauté pan to thinly cover the bottom. Place the pan over high heat, add the garlic and ginger, and sauté. Add the stock, miso and bok choy and cook until the bok choy is slightly softened but not overcooked.

To serve, put a generous helping of the broth in each shallow bowl, distributing the bok choy evenly. Place the salmon on top.

Pacific Halibut with Saffron Leek Sauce & Lemon Aïoli

You can successfully substitute BC sablefish or snapper for the halibut in this dish. Serve some thick rounds of steamed baby potatoes, tiny green beans and batons of carrots or yellow beets.

Cinda Chavich   Serves 8

RECOMMENDED WINE: white blend from southern France (roussanne, marsanne, viognier) or a fruity sauvignon blanc from California

For the aïoli:

2	fresh, large egg yolks	2
3	large cloves garlic, peeled	3
1 tsp.	dry mustard	5 mL
¼ tsp.	salt	1.2 mL
1 cup	good-quality olive oil	240 mL
2 Tbsp.	lemon juice	30 mL
1 Tbsp.	minced lemon zest	15 mL

Combine the egg yolks, garlic, mustard and salt in a blender or food processor. Blend until the garlic is finely minced. With the machine running, slowly add the oil through the feed tube until the aïoli begins to emulsify and thicken. Add the lemon juice and blend quickly to combine. Fold in the lemon zest. Refrigerate in a covered container for up to 3 days.

For the saffron leek sauce:

2 Tbsp.	olive oil	30 mL
1	medium white onion, chopped	1
2	large leeks, white part only, halved and sliced	2
3	cloves garlic, peeled and minced	3
½ cup	dry white wine	120 mL
1	small dried hot chili, crumbled	1
1 cup	canned Roma tomatoes, puréed	240 mL
⅛ tsp.	fennel seed	.5 mL
1	herb bundle (strip orange zest, sprig rosemary and sprig thyme, wrapped in a 3-inch/7.5-cm piece of leek leaf and tied together with string)	1
½ tsp.	lightly crushed saffron threads	2.5 mL
1½ cups	warm fish stock or bottled clam juice	360 mL
1 tsp.	balsamic vinegar	5 mL
1 Tbsp.	cornstarch	15 mL
	salt and freshly ground black pepper to taste	

Salt

Every time I teach a cooking class I feel obliged to give my salt lecture. I tell people I will not tolerate finding table salt (iodized salt) in their cupboards except if they use it in the winter on their sidewalks. There was a time when it was necessary for health reasons to have the iodine in the salt, but we have much easier access to fresh fruits and vegetables now and there are alternatives.

Salt is a cook's most important seasoning. When used properly it works with all the ingredients to heighten the flavour of your food. Like olive oils, I have a few different kinds in my pantry. Do some experimenting of your own. If you are used to table salt, it takes some adjusting to get the right balance with the different salts. Remember, you shouldn't actually taste the salt; if it tastes salty you have used too much.

KOSHER SALT

This is a great all-purpose, free-flowing mined salt containing no additives. The crystals are medium-sized and flaky and can be used both in baking and cooking.

SEL GRIS

This salt is gathered by hand from the salt beds off the western coast of France. It is greyish in colour and the crystals are chunky, although it is available finely ground. It is moister than kosher salt and has more of a mineral taste. It can be used in cooking but is best used after cooking as a finishing touch.

FLEUR DE SEL

Also harvested by hand in the coastal region of France, this is pure and white and has a slightly sweet taste. A little goes a long way and it is usually not used for cooking but as a final garnish to a dish, adding both flavour and a little crunch.

MALDON SALT

Hand-harvested by the same British family for the last 200 years, this salt has a wonderful flaky texture and a mild salty taste. It is so soft it can be crushed between your fingers. This makes a great salt for your salt cellar on the table.

KAREN MILLER

Heat the olive oil in a sauté pan over medium-low heat and cook the onion and leek slowly until very soft and translucent. Add the garlic, wine and chili. Increase the heat and simmer for 3 minutes. Stir in the tomato purée, fennel seed and herb bundle. Crumble the saffron into the fish stock or clam juice and let stand for 5 minutes, then add to the sauce. Simmer, uncovered, for 20 minutes.

Remove the herb bundle and discard. Combine the vinegar and cornstarch to make a paste and whisk into the sauce. Simmer to thicken nicely. Season with salt and pepper. Keep the sauce warm.

For the halibut:

3 Tbsp.	canola or peanut oil	45 mL
8	4-oz. (113-g) halibut fillets, at least 1 inch (2.5 cm) thick, skin on	8
	salt and freshly ground black pepper to taste	
¼ cup	cornstarch	60 mL
	cayenne pepper to taste	

Heat the oil in a large, ovenproof non-stick pan over medium-high heat. Season the fish with salt and pepper and dip the flesh side into cornstarch to coat, shaking off any excess. Sauté the halibut, flesh side down, over medium-high heat for 2 minutes, or until crisp and golden on one side. Turn the fish over and place the pan immediately into a preheated 400°F (200°C) oven to finish cooking, about 5 to 8 minutes, depending on the thickness of the fillets. Be careful not to overcook the halibut as it is a lean fish and can dry out quickly.

Serve the fish in a pool of sauce, topped with a little additional sauce, a generous dollop of aïoli and a dusting of cayenne.

Roasted SALMON Fillets with MANGO Chili Glaze

This is the recipe I recommend to friends when they ask for an easy way to prepare salmon. It is great for crowds because the glaze can be made in advance and the salmon pieces prepared ahead of time and cooked at the last minute. Roasting the salmon at a high heat in the oven could not be easier and this recipe produces great results every time. Even the least adventurous seem to enjoy the sweet and sour heat the glaze gives to the salmon. In the summertime I add freshly chopped peaches to the glaze and you could certainly add chopped mangos anytime. This goes wonderfully with grilled vegetables and a simple couscous salad.

RECOMMENDED WINE:
big, fruity California viognier

Karen Miller

Serves 6

6	6-oz. (170-g) salmon fillets	6
1/2 cup	butter, melted	120 mL
1/2 cup	honey	120 mL
4 Tbsp.	Basil's Fire and Brimstone Hot Gourmet Pepper Sauce, "Mild" version	60 mL
	salt and freshly ground black pepper to taste	

Place the salmon on a baking tray skin side down. Combine the butter, honey and hot sauce, and brush over the salmon. Refrigerate until the glaze has set. This can be done up to 8 hours ahead.

Preheat the oven to 450°F (230°C). Just before baking, salt and pepper the salmon. Bake for about 8 minutes (2 minutes less if the salmon pieces are thin and 2 minutes more if they are really thick). Remove from the oven and serve immediately or at room temperature.

Note: When I first started making this honey glaze I used a good-quality Mexican chili powder instead of the hot sauce. But Basil's Fire and Brimstone Hot Gourmet Pepper Sauce astounds me with its freshness and its beautiful balance of heat and flavour (it also has no garlic in it, which is great once in a while). It is made in Alberta and is available at most specialty food stores. Be brave if you try the "Hot" version. It is really spicy and does not impart the same subtleness to the dish.

Hazelnut & Pecan Roasted Grouper

RECOMMENDED WINE:
Italian sauvignon/garganega blend (has nut-like qualities) or Canadian pinot gris

The nuts in this dish have a surprisingly subtle flavour that complements the fish well. There are many great substitutes for this dish if you don't care for grouper. Sea bass is one of my favourites.

SERVES 6   JUDY WOOD

½ cup	whole hazelnuts	120 mL
½ cup	whole pecans	120 mL
½ cup	grated Parmesan cheese	120 mL
2	cloves garlic, minced	2
1 Tbsp.	fresh thyme	15 mL
½ tsp.	freshly ground black pepper	2.5 mL
½ tsp.	salt	2.5 mL
2 Tbsp.	butter, melted	30 mL
2 Tbsp.	olive oil	30 mL
6	6-oz. (170-g) grouper fillets	6

Preheat the oven to 350°F (175°C).

Place the nuts on a baking sheet and toast for 5 minutes. Remove from the oven and coarsely chop or crush them. (An easy way to crush nuts is to press a heavy frying pan firmly down onto them.) Transfer the nuts into a bowl and add the Parmesan, garlic, thyme, pepper, salt and butter.

Heat the olive oil in an ovenproof frying pan over medium heat. Add the fillets, skin side up, and cook until golden brown, about 3 minutes. Remove from the heat and flip the fillets over. Generously coat each fillet with the nut mixture. Place the pan in the oven and bake for 7 minutes.

Grilled SALMON with Sweet SOY Glaze & MILLET Hot Pot

Millet is a little yellow grain that's most often relegated to bird feed. But toasted and simply steamed it has a lovely nutty flavour that works perfectly with a pot of Asian greens. The simple soy-glazed salmon makes a perfect counterpoint to this unique grain dish. Look for millet in health food stores.

CINDA CHAVICH

SERVES 4

4	5-oz. (140-g) boneless salmon fillet pieces, skin on	4
	canola oil	
	salt and white pepper to taste	
2 Tbsp.	butter	30 mL
2 Tbsp.	honey	30 mL
2 Tbsp.	dark soy sauce	30 mL
¼ tsp.	hot Asian chili paste	1.2 mL
2 tsp.	oyster sauce	10 mL
1 recipe	Millet Hot Pot	1 recipe

For presentation, cut each portion of fish into two pieces. Rub the skin side of the fish with a little canola oil to prevent it from sticking to the grill. Season the flesh side with salt and white pepper. Set aside.

Heat the butter, honey and soy sauce together in a small saucepan. Simmer until smooth and thick. Stir in the chili paste and oyster sauce and cool.

Brush the flesh side of the salmon liberally with the sauce. Preheat the barbecue to medium-high heat and brush the grill with canola oil. Place the fish, skin side down, on the grill. Cover the barbecue and cook until the fish is barely cooked through, about 10 minutes per inch (2.5 cm) thickness. Brush the fish with more sauce two or three times during cooking.

To serve, place a mound of millet and vegetables in each of 4 shallow rimmed soup bowls, and arrange 2 pieces of grilled salmon over each portion.

RECOMMENDED WINE:
Australian semillon/ chardonnay blend or fruity California viognier

SOY SAUCE

Soy sauce is a naturally fermented product of roasted soybeans and a grain, usually wheat, that is aged for up to two years. The first function of soy sauce was as a food preservative, but it is also a highly nutritious and easily digested protein concentrate. There are both light and dark soy sauces. Dark soy is aged longer and, towards the end of the process, molasses is added. It has a thicker consistency and caramel-like flavour. Light soy has a thin consistency and is more salty than the dark variety. Reach for the dark soy sauce when preparing hearty dishes, particularly ones with red meat, and use light soy sauce for more delicate preparations and for dipping sauces. Mushroom soy is flavoured with straw mushrooms and can be used where a dark soy sauce is called for. Tamari is a rich, dark sauce made, ideally, with no wheat, although most tamari is made with some wheat. Both can be found in whole food stores.

GAIL NORTON

Millet Hot Pot

Serves 4

3/4 cup	hulled millet seeds	180 mL
2 Tbsp.	vegetable oil	30 mL
2	cloves garlic, minced	2
2 tsp.	minced fresh ginger	10 mL
2 cups	chopped gai lan (Chinese broccoli)	480 mL
6	baby bok choy, stems sliced and leaves shredded and reserved	6
1	red bell pepper, seeded and chopped	1
1 Tbsp.	Indonesian sweet soy sauce (kecap manis) or teriyaki sauce	15 mL
1 1/2 cups	chicken stock	360 mL
1 tsp.	hot chili sauce	5 mL
4	green onions, cut into 2-inch (5-cm) pieces	4
1 tsp.	sesame oil	5 mL
2 Tbsp.	chopped Thai basil or fresh mint	30 mL
1/4 cup	coarsely chopped roasted cashews	60 mL

Stir the millet in a large dry sauté pan over medium-high heat until the seeds are golden and begin to pop, about 5 minutes. Remove from the heat and set aside.

Heat the oil in a wok or saucepan over medium-high heat and stir-fry the garlic and ginger together for 30 seconds. Add the gai lan, bok choy stems and red pepper and stir-fry for 2 minutes. Cover and steam for 2 minutes longer.

Stir in the soy sauce, chicken stock and chili sauce and bring to a boil. Add the toasted millet, then cover the pot, reduce the heat to low and simmer for 15 to 20 minutes. Remove from the heat and stir in the reserved bok choy leaves and the green onions. Let the pan stand, covered, for 10 minutes longer to steam the millet.

Fluff the millet with a fork and stir in the sesame oil and basil or mint. Sprinkle with cashew nuts.

CHICKEN BREAST WITH PORTOBELLO MUSHROOMS & TRUFFLES IN PHYLLO

Truffles are like gold. They are sometimes available fresh, but can be purchased in jars at specialty stores. If you leave them out of this recipe, you won't have that golden flavour, but even without truffles, this dish is fabulous. Serve it with a mixed green salad.

RECOMMENDED WINE: full-bodied white Burgundy or Rhône

JUDY WOOD

SERVES 6

3	whole boneless skinless chicken breasts, cut into thin short strips (6 halves)	3
2 Tbsp.	butter	30 mL
½	small onion, finely chopped	½
2 tsp.	minced garlic	10 mL
1	large portobello mushroom, thickly sliced	1
½ cup	dry white wine	120 mL
2 Tbsp.	flour	30 mL
½ cup	chicken stock	120 mL
½ cup	whipping cream	120 mL
1 tsp.	fresh thyme	5 mL
1	dark truffle, sliced	1
	salt and freshly ground black pepper to taste	
12	sheets phyllo pastry	12
¼ cup	butter, melted	60 mL

Heat a medium frying pan over high heat. Add the chicken and sear until browned.

In the same pan, melt the butter over medium-high heat. Add the onion and garlic and sauté for about 5 minutes. Add the mushroom and sauté for 5 to 8 minutes, until brown. Add the wine and cook until the volume is reduced by half, about 5 to 7 minutes. Add the flour, stirring it in well, and cook for 1 to 2 minutes. Add the stock and cook for 20 minutes, allowing the sauce to thicken. Add the cream, thyme and truffle and simmer for 3 to 5 minutes. Season with salt and pepper. Set the mixture aside.

Preheat the oven to 350°F (175°C).

Place 1 sheet of phyllo on your work surface with the short side at the top and bottom. (Be sure to keep the remaining phyllo covered with waxed paper, then a damp towel.) Brush a thin layer of melted butter on the phyllo. Place another sheet of phyllo over top and brush with butter. Using a knife, cut the phyllo in half lengthwise. Place a large scoop of the chicken and mushroom mixture at the bottom of each phyllo rectangle. Lift one bottom corner up and over the mixture to make a triangle shape. Fold the wrapped mixture up (so the bottom of the strip is squared off), then across to form a triangle again. Continue folding to the end of the rectangle. Repeat until all the filling has been used. Place the parcels on a baking sheet. Bake for about 15 minutes, until brown.

ROASTED CHICKEN WITH GINGER MUSTARD SAUCE

The flavour combination in this dish was inspired by a recipe originating with Charlie Trotter, a Chicago chef famous for his complex, artful creations. The intensity of the preserved ginger and the mustard satisfies those yin-yang cravings of sweet and sour. This easy-to-prepare dish is an elegant, entertaining dinner plate. Serve it with decadent mashed potatoes and crisp green beans for great contrasts in texture and flavour.

RECOMMENDED WINE:
fruity, unoaked chardonnay from Australia or California

KAREN MILLER

SERVES 4

2	whole boneless chicken breasts, skin on, cut in half	2
1 Tbsp.	butter	15 mL
	salt and freshly ground black pepper to taste	
1 Tbsp.	fresh thyme leaves	15 mL
2 cups	white wine	480 mL
2 Tbsp.	whole grain mustard	30 mL
1/4 cup	preserved ginger in syrup, chopped	60 mL
1/4 cup	butter	60 mL
1 Tbsp.	rice wine vinegar	15 mL

Preheat the oven to 400°F (200°C). Smother the skin of the chicken with butter and sprinkle with salt and pepper. Scatter the thyme leaves over the chicken breasts. Place in a roasting pan and bake for 20 minutes.

While the chicken is roasting make the sauce. Place the wine in a saucepan over medium-high heat and cook until it's reduced by about half. Whisk in the remaining ingredients. To serve, spoon the sauce over the chicken breasts.

BALSAMIC DUCK BREAST WITH THREE-LILY CONFIT

RECOMMENDED WINE:
California or Pacific
Northwest zinfandel, merlot
or cabernet sauvignon

Before you start challenging me on my unusual ingredients, onions are members of the lily family. This recipe uses 3 different onions to make a heavenly accompaniment to serve alongside the duck. Duck has always been one of my favourite meat choices for entertaining. It's easy to pair with wine, has lots of flavour and is an unusual entrée for many guests. The balsamic vinegar gives the duck a lovely glaze and a slight sweetness. Serve with scalloped potatoes and steamed fresh green beans.

JANET WEBB

SERVES 4

2	whole boneless, skinless duck breasts, cut in half and excess fat removed	2
	salt and freshly ground black pepper to taste	
2 Tbsp.	olive oil	30 mL
3 Tbsp.	unsalted butter	45 mL
1/4 cup	balsamic vinegar	60 mL
3 Tbsp.	olive oil	45 mL
2	large red onions, thinly sliced	2
1	leek, white part only, thinly sliced	1
2	shallots, minced	2
1/4 cup	balsamic vinegar	60 mL
1/2 cup	chicken stock	120 mL

Preheat the oven to 375°F (190°C). Season the duck breasts with salt and pepper. Oil a baking dish large enough to hold the duck breasts with the 2 Tbsp. (30 mL) oil. Melt the butter in a medium sauté pan. Sear the duck breasts over high heat until golden brown, about 2 minutes on each side. Transfer to the prepared dish and drizzle 1/4 cup (60 mL) balsamic vinegar over the breasts. Cover with foil and bake for 15 to 20 minutes for medium.

Using the same sauté pan, heat the 3 Tbsp. (45 mL) olive oil over medium heat. Add the onions, leek and shallot, and sauté for 15 minutes, stirring occasionally, until they begin to caramelize. Add the remaining 1/4 cup (60 mL) balsamic vinegar and continue to cook until thickened. Add the chicken stock and continue to cook until the liquid has reduced and has a sauce-like consistency, about 10 to 15 minutes. Keep warm.

Remove the duck breasts from the oven and let rest for 5 minutes. Slice on the diagonal and arrange on serving plates. Spoon the onion confit over or alongside the breasts.

Duck Legs with Cabbage & Tomatoes

This is my all-time favourite winter dish. I get so excited when the weather turns even the slightest bit cold, as it is an excuse to make this duck leg dish. If there are any leftovers I add some lentils and stock and have a delicious lentil stew.

GAIL NORTON

RECOMMENDED WINE: fleshy Côtes du Rhône, or softer Languedoc blend

SERVES 4 TO 6

4–6	duck legs	4–6
1 Tbsp.	dried thyme	15 mL
	kosher salt and freshly ground black pepper to taste	
6 Tbsp.	olive oil	90 mL
3	large onions, sliced	3
4	cloves garlic, minced	4
1	head cabbage (preferably organic), finely sliced	1
4	large tomatoes, chopped	4
1/4 cup	balsamic vinegar	60 mL
6 cups	veal or chicken stock	1.5 L

Sprinkle the duck legs with the thyme, salt and pepper and allow to sit at room temperature for at least 30 minutes and up to 1 hour (this step can also be done the night before and the duck refrigerated).

Preheat the oven to 400°F (200°C). Place a cookie sheet in the oven and when it is very hot add the duck legs, skin side down. Cook for about 30 minutes, until much of the fat has been rendered off and the skin is crispy. Turn the legs over, and cook 5 minutes longer. Set aside.

Cover the bottom of a large ovenproof pan over high heat with the olive oil. Reduce the heat to medium-high and sauté the onions and garlic at a brisk pace for several minutes, until they are starting to soften but not browned. Add the cabbage and stir to coat it in the olive oil and onion mixture; add more oil if necessary to keep the mixture moist. Reduce the heat to low, cover the pan and cook the mixture very slowly, stirring occasionally, for at least 30 minutes and for as long as 1 hour. The longer it cooks, the more luscious the texture is.

Stir in the tomatoes and balsamic vinegar. Add the duck legs and stock to the pan. Put in the oven and bake for at least 1 1/2 hours and up to 3 hours. It is done when the duck is very tender.

PORTOBELLO
MUSHROOM RISOTTO

RECOMMENDED WINE:
big, fruity dolcetto or
primitivo from Italy

ARBORIO, VIALONE NANO,
CARNAROLI

You decide to make a
risotto but what rice
should you use? There are
several types to choose
from and each provides
different risotto character-
istics. The three most
readily available are
Arborio, Vialone Nano and
Carnaroli. Arborio has a
large, plump grain and
produces a stickier risotto
due to a high soft starch
content. It is great for
more compact risotto.
Vialone Nano is a stubby,
small grain with a high
starch content, but it's a
different, tougher kind of
starch than Arborio. It
doesn't soften easily in
cooking and offers a
distinct resistance to the
bite. It is ideal for risottos.
Carnaroli was developed
by a Milanese rice grower
who crossed Vialone with
a Japanese strain. It is
more expensive than the
others, but Marcella Hazan,
doyenne of Italian cooking,
recommends it over the
others. The kernel has the
soft starch that dissolves,
but it also contains a
tougher starch than the
other varieties so that it
cooks to a firm
consistency.

GAIL NORTON

More traditionally known as Risotta alla Milanese, the portobello
mushrooms are a wonderful addition to this dish. My friend
Connie, an expat Calgarian who has lived in Rome for years,
whips this dish up without measuring anything—true Italian flare.
For starch addicts like myself, there is nothing better than risotto
to satisfy your hunger.

SERVES 6   RHONDDA SIEBENS

4¼ cups	chicken stock (or vegetable stock)	1 L
3 Tbsp.	olive oil	45 mL
1 cup	portobello mushrooms, thinly sliced	240 mL
	sea salt and freshly ground black pepper to taste	
⅔ cup	butter	160 mL
2	medium onions, peeled and finely chopped	2
1¼ cups	Arborio rice	300 mL
⅓ cup	dry white wine (or dry white vermouth)	80 mL
	pinch saffron	
6 oz.	Parmesan cheese, freshly grated	170 g

Heat the stock and have ready at a simmer.

Heat 1 Tbsp. (15 mL) of the olive oil in a very hot pan. Add the
mushrooms and cook for 1 minute. Season with salt and pepper
and continue to cook for approximately 2 more minutes. Set
aside.

In a heavy saucepan, heat the remaining 2 Tbsp. (30 mL) olive oil
and half of the butter over medium heat. Add the onion and
sauté until soft, approximately 15 minutes. Add the rice and stir
for 2 or 3 minutes until it is coated with the butter. Add the white
wine and keep stirring as it cooks into the rice.

Add your first ladle of stock and reduce the heat to a simmer.
Add the mushrooms at this time and keep stirring. Continue to
add the stock at intervals, stirring and allowing the stock to be
absorbed before adding more. After 15 to 20 minutes, nearly all
the stock will have been absorbed. Check the seasoning and add
salt and pepper if desired. Remove from the heat and stir in the
remaining butter and the grated Parmesan, reserving a bit of
cheese for garnish. Serve immediately.

Israeli Couscous with Lamb, Vegetables & Chickpeas

This is one of those comforting but slightly exotic dishes to serve family-style or as part of a Moroccan-inspired meal—the kind you can cook after work with ingredients from the pantry and a little ground lamb that you pick up in the supermarket freezer. Use Israeli couscous if you can find it. It's much larger than the more common instant couscous—the size of a small pea—or substitute a tiny pasta like orzo. With chickpeas but no lamb, this nicely spiced combination makes a satisfying vegetarian meal.

RECOMMENDED WINE:
full-bodied Cru Beaujolais
or fruity Languedoc blend

CINDA CHAVICH

SERVES 4

1 Tbsp.	olive oil	15 mL
3/4 lb.	ground or chopped lean lamb	340 g
2 tsp.	minced fresh ginger	10 mL
2	cloves garlic, minced	2
1 tsp.	ground cumin	5 mL
1/2 tsp.	paprika	2.5 mL
1/4 tsp.	ground cinnamon	1.2 mL
1	red bell pepper, chopped	1
1	large onion, quartered and thinly sliced	1
2	medium carrots, chopped	2
1	medium zucchini, cubed	1
1 tsp.	Asian chili paste	5 mL
2–2 1/2 cups	vegetable or chicken broth	480–600 mL
1/8 tsp.	saffron powder	.5 mL
1/4 tsp.	salt	1.2 mL
1/4 cup	raisins or dried currants	60 mL
1	14-oz. (398-mL) can chickpeas, rinsed and drained (optional)	1
1 cup	large Israeli or whole grain medium couscous	240 mL
1/4 cup	chopped cilantro, for garnish	60 mL

Heat the oil in a large sauté pan. Add the ground lamb and break it up into chunks. Sauté over medium-high heat until nicely browned, about 10 to 15 minutes. Remove the lamb from the pan and drain the fat.

Add the ginger, garlic, cumin, paprika and cinnamon to the pan and toast the spices for 30 seconds. Add the red pepper, onion, carrots and zucchini to the pan and sauté until the vegetables are soft, about 10 minutes. Stir in the chili paste.

Combine the broth and saffron and set aside to steep for a few minutes.

Return the lamb to the pan and stir in the saffron broth, salt, raisins or currants and chickpeas (if using). Bring to a boil over high heat. Stir in the couscous, cover the pan, reduce the heat to low and simmer for 15 to 20 minutes. Add more broth if the mixture seems too dry. Remove from the heat and let stand for 8 to 10 minutes, until most of the liquid has been absorbed and the couscous granules are cooked through.

Mound the couscous on a serving platter. Scatter the chopped cilantro over top and serve immediately.

Roasted Vegetable Tortelli with Thyme Butter

Homemade, handmade pasta has always been one of the most popular items I have ever put on a menu or served to guests at home. A favourite entertaining idea is to get the guests involved with the making of the pasta. Be sure to have plenty of Chianti and Pavarotti around for inspiration.

RECOMMENDED WINE: rich, leathery Chianti Riserva!

SHELLEY ROBINSON

SERVES 6 AS A MAIN COURSE WITH EXTRA TO FREEZE

1 recipe	Pasta Dough (page 161)	1 recipe
½	yellow bell pepper, finely diced	½
½	red bell pepper, finely diced	½
1	small zucchini, finely diced	1
1	small eggplant, finely diced	1
1	medium carrot, finely diced	1
½	onion, finely diced	½
1	stalk celery, finely diced	1
¼ cup	olive oil	60 mL
2	cloves garlic, minced	2
1 cup	ricotta cheese	240 mL
½ cup	grated Parmesan cheese	120 mL
2 Tbsp.	chopped garlic	30 mL
⅔ cup	fine bread crumbs	160 mL
2 Tbsp.	chopped fresh thyme	30 mL
	salt and freshly ground black pepper to taste	
½ cup	white wine	120 mL
1	lemon, juice only	1
1 Tbsp.	finely diced shallots	15 mL
2 Tbsp.	chopped fresh thyme	30 mL
½ lb.	cold butter, cut into small cubes	225 g
	fresh thyme sprigs, for garnish	

Prepare the pasta dough and allow to rest in the refrigerator. Prepare the diced vegetables, keeping them in separate bowls.

Add a little of the ¼ cup (60 mL) oil to a very hot sauté pan and sauté each vegetable individually until nicely browned, seasoning with salt and pepper as you go. Add more oil to the pan as needed for each individual sauté. When sautéeing the last batch of vegetables, add the minced garlic halfway through. Put all of the sautéed vegetables together in a mixing bowl and allow to cool. Stir in the ricotta, Parmesan, 2 Tbsp. (30 mL) chopped garlic, bread crumbs and thyme. Season with salt and pepper.

To make the pasta, cut the dough into thirds. Flatten one portion of the dough and begin to feed it through the largest setting of the pasta machine. Continue this process, making the opening smaller each time you pass it through, until you have a long piece about ¼ inch (.6 cm) thick. Using a 2-Tbsp. (30-mL) scoop, place mounds of filling in a row down the centre of the sheet. Spray lightly with water and fold the pasta over to enclose the filling. Press down firmly around the filling to remove any air bubbles and to seal the edges of the pasta. Use a pastry wheel to cut triangle-shaped pieces. Place the finished tortelli on a floured tray, and repeat with the remaining dough. If freezing, allow to dry for several hours on each side, before placing the tray into the freezer. Once frozen, the tortelli can be placed in airtight containers and stored in the freezer.

Bring a large pot of salted water to a boil. Place the frozen or freshly made tortelli into the water and cook for 6 to 8 minutes, or until al dente.

For the sauce, put the wine, lemon juice and shallots into a small pot and bring to a simmer. Add the remaining 2 Tbsp. (30 mL) chopped thyme and reduce the heat to low. Whisk in the butter a little at a time and season if required.

To serve, place 5 to 6 pieces of the tortelli on each plate and spoon the sauce over each. Garnish with fresh thyme sprigs.

MISO-BRAISED MUSHROOMS ON A POLENTA BED

Among a bunch of friends who were coming for dinner, two were vegetarians. I didn't want to make a fuss and have two separate menus, so I set myself the challenge of serving a meal where no one would miss the other food groups. This dish worked so well that nobody even noticed they were eating vegetarian, and it has become part of my repertoire. Look for polenta-cut cornmeal in specialty and large grocery stores. You can substitute regular cornmeal at a pinch, but the texture will not be as pleasing.

RECOMMENDED WINE: rich, red Rhône blend or spicier Cru Beaujolais Moulin-à-Vent

GAIL NORTON

SERVES 8 TO 10

1	large eggplant, chopped	1
2 Tbsp.	lemon juice	30 mL
2 tsp.	salt	10 mL
2 Tbsp.	olive oil	30 mL
2 Tbsp.	butter	30 mL
1	medium onion, chopped	1
2	cloves garlic, minced	2
1	large portobello mushroom, chopped	1
1 lb.	cultivated mushrooms, chopped	450 g
1 lb.	various exotic mushrooms, chopped	450 g
2 tsp.	grated fresh ginger	10 mL
3 Tbsp.	mirin	45 mL
1 tsp.	soy sauce	5 mL
1 Tbsp.	dark miso	15 mL
1 Tbsp.	white miso	15 mL
4 cups	stock or water	1 L
1 Tbsp.	kosher salt	15 mL
1½ cups	polenta-cut cornmeal	360 mL
2 Tbsp.	butter	30 mL
½ cup	grated Parmesan cheese (optional)	120 mL
	salt and freshly ground black pepper to taste	

Miso, a fermented soybean paste used in Japanese cookery, is one of those underused ingredients—a dollop goes a long way in making this dish (and any other stewy creations) rich and luscious, with a slight nutty flavour. The darker the miso, the stronger the flavour; think of it like stock—dark miso is akin to beef stock and white miso is like chicken stock. It will keep virtually indefinitely in the refrigerator.

GAIL NORTON

Bring a pot of salted water to a boil. Add the eggplant, lemon juice and 2 tsp. (10 mL) salt to the water and simmer, making sure there is enough water to cover the eggplant at all times. Cook until the eggplant is just tender, about 8 to 10 minutes. Drain and set aside.

In a large frying pan, heat the olive oil and 2 Tbsp. (30 mL) of butter. Sauté the onion and garlic on high heat until the liquids from the onions are released, about 5 minutes, stirring often. Turn the heat to very low, cover and continue to cook for another 15 minutes. Add all the mushrooms and the ginger. Cook uncovered until the liquid from the mushrooms has been released, then continue to cook until the liquid is reduced and the mushrooms are very soft. Add the mirin, soy sauce and miso pastes, turn the heat down and gently simmer for about 5 minutes. Add the cooked eggplant and continue simmering while you prepare the polenta. Make sure that the mixture does not become too dry— add a little water or stock to ensure that it does not scorch.

Bring the stock or water to a boil in a large saucepan and add the kosher salt. Lower the heat to medium and slowly add the cornmeal, stirring constantly. Continue to simmer, stirring periodically, until it is thick enough for the spoon to stand in the polenta, or until the grains have softened. Add the 2 Tbsp. (30 mL) butter and the cheese (if using) and mix well. Season with salt and pepper.

To serve, place a generous spoonful of polenta on each plate and top with a portion of the miso-mushroom mixture.

INDIVIDUAL LOBSTER LASAGNAS WITH TWO CHEESES

This was a meal I created for an elegant dinner one Christmas Eve. It's a rich and decadent dish, but it's perfect for celebrating.

CINDA CHAVICH

RECOMMENDED WINE: Sancerre or Pouilly Fumé from the Loire or a racy Chablis

SERVES 4

1	medium bulb fennel, trimmed	1
1 Tbsp.	olive oil	15 mL
1 Tbsp.	butter	15 mL
1	medium white onion, minced	1
1	medium carrot, finely diced	1
1	clove garlic, minced	1
2 Tbsp.	cognac	30 mL
1 cup	chopped fresh or canned tomatoes	240 mL
1 Tbsp.	tomato paste	15 mL
1 cup	fish stock or lobster stock	240 mL
1/2 cup	dry white wine	120 mL
1/4 cup	whipping cream	60 mL
2 cups	cooked lobster meat, chopped	480 mL
	salt and white pepper to taste	
1 lb.	fresh lasagna sheets, cut into 16 rectangles, 3 x 5 inches (7.5 x 12.5 cm)	450 g
4 oz.	shredded dry Friulano cheese	115 g
1/4 cup	shredded Parmesan cheese	60 mL

Finely slice the fennel bulb, reserving some of the fronds for garnish.

Heat the oil and butter in a deep skillet over medium-high heat and sauté the onion, carrot and fennel for 5 minutes, until almost tender. Add the garlic and cognac and simmer until most of the liquid has evaporated. Stir in the tomatoes, tomato paste, stock and wine, and simmer until the sauce has reduced by half. Add the cream and simmer 5 minutes longer, until the sauce is thickened nicely. Stir in the lobster meat, season with salt and pepper, and remove the sauce from the heat. Keep warm.

You'll need about 5 lbs. (2.25 kg) of live lobster to make 2 cups (480 mL) of cooked meat. Steam or boil live lobsters for 12 to 15 minutes. Crack the shells when cool and reserve the meat (the shells are great for making lobster stock for this dish). Alternately, use frozen precooked lobster tails or canned, frozen lobster meat (you don't get the shells for stock but you save a lot of time and the quality of the frozen canned product is very good). For a mixed seafood lasagna, substitute some scallops and prawns for the lobster in the sauce.

Bring a pot of salted water to a boil and cook the pasta until just cooked through but still al dente, about 2 to 3 minutes. Drain and chill in cold water, then drain again.

Combine the two cheeses. Preheat the oven to 375°F (190°C).

To make individual lasagnas, place a little of the sauce into the bottom of four ovenproof dishes. Top with a sheet of pasta and a layer of sauce. Sprinkle lightly with cheese and add another layer of pasta. Continue layering sauce, cheese and pasta until each individual lasagna has four layers, ending with pasta. Sprinkle the tops with more cheese. Bake the lasagnas for 7 to 8 minutes, just until bubbling and beginning to brown. Garnish each with reserved fennel fronds and serve immediately.

PAPPARDELLE WITH TRUFFLES & CREAM

All over Italy pasta is eaten as a first course, most often at mid-day. Fresh pasta became part of this first course in the form of dumplings added to soups, later called ravioli. In Tuscany, wide hand-cut pappardelle are used with a great range of rich sauces, often with wild mushrooms from the region. This is a quick and easy way to enjoy fresh pasta as a first plate or in larger portions as a meal. The make-ahead truffle butter keeps well in the freezer. Be sure and wrap it well, as it does have a permeating aroma. Leftover pasta dough will keep in the fridge for up to 5 days.

RECOMMENDED WINE: needs acidity to counteract the richness ... Chablis, French viognier

SHELLEY ROBINSON   SERVES 6 AS A FIRST PLATE, OR 4 AS A MAIN COURSE

4 cups	whipping cream	950 mL
1/2 recipe	Pasta Dough (see page 161)	1/2 recipe
1/3 cup	Truffle Butter (see page 161)	80 mL
1 Tbsp.	freshly cracked black pepper	15 mL
2 tsp.	kosher salt	10 mL
2 Tbsp.	truffle oil	30 mL
1 cup	freshly grated Parmesan cheese	240 mL

In a large saucepan, heat the whipping cream over medium heat, allowing the cream to simmer, but not boil. You want the cream to reduce by 1/3 and in doing so it will thicken.

Meanwhile prepare the pasta maker and cut your pasta dough into thirds. Flatten the dough with the heel of your hand and begin to feed it through the largest setting of the machine. Continue this procedure, making the opening of the pasta maker smaller each time you pass it through, until you have a long piece about 1/4 inch (.6 cm) thick. With a pastry cutter, begin at one end and cut a piece 1 inch (2.5 cm) wide, rolling towards the other end. If you like, give the strand a ragged edge by rolling the cutter from side to side as you move it towards the other end. Place the finished pappardelle on baking sheets dusted with flour until you are ready to cook. Repeat with the remaining dough.

Cook the completed pasta in a large pot of salted water for 3 to 5 minutes. While the pasta is cooking, whisk the truffle butter into the cream and season with some of the pepper and salt. Drain the pasta well and return it to the pot. Quickly pour the cream sauce over the pasta and toss to ensure that it is well coated.

Divide the pasta among the appropriate bowls and finish with the remaining salt and pepper, a drizzle of truffle oil and finally the Parmesan cheese.

Asian-Spiced Salmon with Braised Bok Choy (p. 139)

Tuna Burger with Cucumber Sake Ribbons & Wasabi Mayo (p. 136)

Wrapped Chicken with Sage & Prosciutto (p. 127) and Braised
Fennel with Rosemary Honey & Balsamic Vinegar (p. 179)

Israeli Couscous with Lamb, Vegetables & Chickpeas (p. 152)

Truffle Butter

Makes about 2 cups (480 mL)

2	fresh or jarred black or white truffles	2
1 lb.	unsalted butter, softened	450 g
2 Tbsp.	truffle oil	30 mL

If using fresh truffles, clean them with a soft brush to remove any dirt. Cut the truffles into quarters and place in the food processor with the butter and truffle oil. Process until the truffles have been reduced to the size of cracked black pepper or smaller. Roll the butter in plastic wrap to form a log and place in the freezer. Each time you need some butter, simply cut a chunk off.

Pasta Dough

1 lb.	all-purpose flour, plus extra for dusting	450 g
5	large eggs	5
1 Tbsp.	salt	15 mL
$\frac{1}{4}$–$\frac{1}{3}$ cup	water	60–80 mL

Place the flour and salt in the bowl of a food processor. With the motor running, add the eggs one at a time. The mixture should resemble coarse bread crumbs. With the machine running, add water a little at a time until the dough forms a ball. Remove the dough and knead it on a clean flat surface until it is smooth. Form into a log and flatten slightly. Refrigerate the dough for at least 2 hours before using.

The dough can be frozen or kept tightly wrapped in the refrigerator for up to 3 days.

RADIATORE with ROASTED GOLDEN NUGGET SQUASH & HAZELNUT SAGE PESTO

This makes a good vegetarian first course or supper. Radiatore is a "radiator-shaped" pasta with lots of ridges to catch the nutty sage pesto sauce. Feel free to substitute fusili or other short pasta. You can also serve a dollop of this pesto on roasted pieces of golden nugget squash as a side dish. Just remove the seeds, cut the squash into halves, quarters or wedges, brush with oil and roast—they're small and make a nice addition to a fall supper of roasted free-range chicken.

RECOMMENDED WINE: buttery chardonnay from California or a Pacific Northwest pinot noir

CINDA CHAVICH

SERVES 6 AS A FIRST COURSE

3	golden nugget or small acorn squash	3
3 Tbsp.	olive oil	45 mL
	salt to taste	
1 lb.	radiatore or other short pasta	450 g
1 recipe	Hazelnut Sage Pesto	1 recipe
1/3 cup	cream (optional)	80 mL
	extra sage leaves, curls of Parmesan cheese and cold-pressed canola or hazelnut oil, for garnish	

Cut the squash in half and remove the seeds, scraping them out with a small spoon. Remove the peel and cut the flesh into 1-inch (2.5-cm) cubes. Place the squash in a baking dish and drizzle with the oil, tossing to coat. Season with salt and bake at 400°F (200°C) for 20 to 30 minutes, until the squash is tender and starting to brown.

Cook the pasta in boiling salted water until al dente. Drain well and stir in the pesto and cream (if using). Add the hot roasted squash and toss. Arrange the pasta in shallow bowls, topped with a sprig of sage, a shard of shaved Parmesan and a drizzle of nutty cold-pressed canola or hazelnut oil.

Hazelnuts (a.k.a filberts) are one of my favourite nuts, rich and sweet when perfectly fresh. You should toast your hazelnuts to enhance their nutty flavour. You can also buy pre-roasted and peeled hazelnuts at Italian markets. Or feel free to substitute toasted almonds (skin on) in this recipe.

HAZELNUT SAGE PESTO

MAKES 2½ CUPS (600 mL)

⅓ cup	chopped fresh sage leaves	80 mL
⅓ cup	good-quality olive oil	80 mL
¼ cup	canola oil	60 mL
½ cup	toasted hazelnuts (see page 216)	120 mL
2	large cloves garlic, minced	2
	pinch grated nutmeg	
	pinch freshly ground black pepper	
½ tsp.	salt	2.5 mL
1½ cups	freshly grated Parmesan cheese	360 mL

Combine the sage leaves, oils, hazelnuts, garlic, pepper, nutmeg and salt in a food processor and pulse until the nuts are finely chopped and the pesto is smooth. Stir in the Parmesan cheese.

Herb Tortellini with Fresh Tomato Sauce

Always remember that won ton or gyoza wrappers will expand more than fresh pasta. The process sounds tricky but it's not really. Don't be afraid to change the filling to suit your own taste preferences. Perhaps add a little grilled chicken! It's worth the venture to make it your own.

RECOMMENDED WINE: soft, fruity sangiovese, Chianti or primitivo

JUDY WOOD

SERVES 6

1 cup	ricotta cheese	240 mL
1	egg yolk	1
1 cup	Parmesan cheese	240 mL
3/4 cup	mixed fresh basil and parsley	180 mL
	salt and freshly ground black pepper to taste	
1/4 tsp.	ground nutmeg (optional)	1.2 mL
1	package won ton or gyoza wrappers	1
1 recipe	Fresh Tomato Sauce	1 recipe
1/3 cup	grated Parmesan cheese	80 mL

Mix the ricotta, egg yolk and Parmesan with a fork until light and creamy. Stir in the basil and parsley and season with salt and pepper. Add nutmeg, if desired.

Place the wrappers on your work surface. Place a generous teaspoon of filling on each square. With a pastry brush, evenly brush a little water on the edges of the wrappers. Fold each square in half diagonally, creating a triangle, making sure all the air is extracted. With the folded edge closest to you, roll it once, away from you. Then bring the two corners into the centre and pinch them together to make the tortellini.

Bring a large pot of salted water to a boil and cook the tortellini for 3 to 4 minutes. Drain the tortellini and toss with the sauce. Sprinkle with the Parmesan and serve immediately.

Fresh Tomato Sauce

MAKES 2 CUPS (480 ML)

4 Tbsp.	olive oil	60 mL
3–4	cloves garlic, minced	3–4
6–8	Roma tomatoes, blanched and peeled (or 2 cups/480 mL canned)	6–8
½ cup	red wine	120 mL
1 cup	chicken stock	240 mL
1 Tbsp.	fresh oregano	15 mL
1 tsp.	fresh thyme	5 mL
3 Tbsp.	fresh parsley	45 mL
	salt and freshly ground black pepper to taste	

Heat the olive oil in a medium saucepan over medium heat. Add the garlic and cook for 2 to 3 minutes. Coarsely chop the tomatoes and add them to the pan. Cook for 2 minutes, then add the wine. Cook for 5 to 10 minutes, until the wine has reduced by about half. Add the chicken stock and simmer for 20 minutes on low heat. Stir in the fresh herbs and season with salt and pepper.

Wild Mushroom Sauce for Pasta

Although this is a favourite sauce with pasta, it is also a great topping for crostini or polenta.

RECOMMENDED WINE: dolcetto or lighter nebbiolo from the Valtellina region in Italy

GAIL NORTON

SERVES 4 TO 6

1 Tbsp.	olive oil	15 mL
2 oz.	thickly cut pancetta, cubed	57 g
4	cloves garlic, minced	4
1	onion, chopped	1
2.2 lbs.	mixed mushrooms, chopped	1 kg
1/4 cup	sherry	60 mL
1 cup	chicken stock	240 mL
1/2 cup	minced parsley	120 mL
1 lb.	fusilli or other pasta	450 g
4 Tbsp.	grated Parmesan or manchego cheese	60 mL
	pinch cayenne	
	salt and freshly ground black pepper to taste	

Heat the olive oil in a sauté pan over high heat. Add the pancetta and sauté until slightly crispy. Remove the pancetta from the pan and set aside. Reduce the heat to medium, add the garlic and onion to the pan and sauté until softened, about 10 minutes. Add the mushrooms and cook until they have released their liquid; continue cooking until all the liquid has evaporated. Add the sherry, stock and parsley. Continue cooking until the sauce is the consistency you want.

Cook the pasta in a large pot of boiling water according to package directions. Drain well.

Just before serving, add the cheese, cayenne, salt and pepper to the sauce. Toss with the pasta.

Basic MARINARA Sauce

RECOMMENDED WINE:
Italian—anything from light, simple Chianti to full-throttled Amarone depending on what you add to the sauce

Having a great tomato sauce around is the inspiration for many last-minute meals in my home; it is also an essential item in most professional kitchens I've worked in. Make the base and then let your imagination take over: add grilled veggies, sauté some spicy sausage, get fresh herbs from the garden, rehydrate some wild mushrooms, use as a pizza sauce or bake with snapper and capers. You get the picture.

MAKES 12 CUPS (3 L)   SHELLEY ROBINSON

1/3 cup	olive oil	80 mL
1	onion, finely chopped	1
8–10	cloves garlic, finely chopped	8–10
2	shallots, finely chopped	2
4	anchovy fillets, rinsed	4
1 Tbsp.	chili flakes (optional)	15 mL
1/2 cup	packed fresh basil leaves, torn	120 mL
1/3 cup	tomato paste	80 mL
2 Tbsp.	ground oregano	30 mL
2 cups	drinkable red wine, not too dry	480 mL
1	100-oz. (3-L) can Italian plum tomatoes	1
	salt and freshly ground black pepper to taste	
1/4 cup	extra virgin olive oil	60 mL

Place the 1/3 cup (80 mL) olive oil in a heavy pot over medium heat. When it's hot, add the onion, garlic and shallots and stir madly until the garlic just starts to colour. Add the anchovies, chili flakes (if using), basil and tomato paste. Cook the mixture until everything is gathered up in the tomato paste and it seems "sticky." Add the oregano. Pour in the red wine slowly while stirring to loosen the mixture up again. Reduce the heat to low. Place a strainer or colander over top of the pot and pour the canned plum tomatoes into it so the juices run through. Squeeze the whole tomatoes with your hand and crush them, then tip the crushed tomatoes into the bubbling mixture below. Continue to stir often as the sauce simmers, and season with salt and pepper a little at a time as the sauce reduces. Cook over low heat until you have the yield and thickness you want to achieve. You can always leave the sauce a little on the runny side if you intend to cook it further at a later date; however, to get the best flavour, it should cook for a minimum of 1 1/2 hours. To finish, stir in the 1/4 cup (60 mL) olive oil and adjust with salt and pepper if necessary.

Cool the sauce in hot sterilized jars. It will keep in the refrigerator for 1 to 2 weeks.

ENTERTAINING:
IT'S ONLY DINNER

The biggest problem with entertaining is expectations. We put too many of them around everything we do these days, so hosting a dinner party is right up there on the stress-o-meter with a root canal for many people.

I admit, I have been among those denizens of the culinary world who have added to this flurry of high food fashion — keen to drape and scape my table in the latest style and create drop dead menus using the hottest new ingredients. But I'm over that now.

It's time to reclaim the dining experience for what it is—a chance to sit and share food, drink and ideas with interesting people with whom you enjoy spending time. Life is too short for anything else.

Yes, I still like to set a nice table—I think the enjoyment of food is as much about eye and aroma appeal as it is about great flavours. I do try to present dishes with a light hand, and a touch of artistry. And I want my meals to have a logical beginning, middle and end, with dishes that work well together and offer enough contrast in flavour, texture and colour to be appealing.

But I refuse to spend days planning and gathering and cooking for every evening that I want to enjoy with friends and family. Occasionally, I will pull out all of the stops. But, mostly, I think we need to chill out and remember that parties are about having fun, and that means fun for everyone, including the cook!

There are several ways to accomplish this easily—one dish extravaganza (think paella, cassoulet or bouillabaisse); the well-engineered pot luck (the host assigns a theme and a course, then each participant knocks themselves out on their own contribution); or the latest in do-it-yourself, interactive eating (you shop and they shuck, sukiyaki, fondue or roll-their-own fajitas or sushi). Everyone eats and has fun. Simple.

It's taken me many years to understand this, but I now know that the stress I once experienced every time I invited people to dinner was of my own making. It was my expectations—not the expectations of my guests—that I was killing myself to meet. This is not an easy lesson to learn but one that I wish everyone would embrace.

Think about it. We are all so busy and overworked these days—the idea that someone is willing to cook for you—and I mean cook almost anything—is amazing. I'm constantly urging my friends to call at 4 o'clock and invite me by for a burger on the grill or anything else that they feel

confident cooking. I'll be there—wine in hand.

And don't worry about failures, mistakes or burnt offerings. If something goes so terribly wrong that you can't save it, order a pizza.

My idea of a great dinner party is one that is so stimulating and fun that I wake up in the morning giddy about the insanity of it all, and find one of the side dishes or appetizers, still chilled and waiting to be served, in the refrigerator. Relax. Enjoy. Fugeddaboudit!

CINDA CHAVICH

Some Cocktail Party Pet Peeves

Nothing is more annoying than being at a cocktail reception with a drink in one hand and being offered an hors d'oeuvre that is the size of lunch for many people in the world. Whether the food is served on a plate or with a cocktail napkin, the servings should be manageable. At a stand-up cocktail party, nothing should be bigger than two small bites.

When it comes to crackers, the choices are numerous, but please discriminate. Vary the size of crackers and the tastes. Do not let the cracker overpower what goes on top. Size matters here too. Big is okay when the cheese platter is set out on a table and guests fix their own. As for served canapés, stick to smaller crackers so jaw surgery is not necessary and a trail of crumbs does not descend upon the recently vacuumed carpet.

Skewers are a great way to serve different types of food, whether plated or with napkins. But skewers are not without their own bad habits. When served on a plate and the guest is to remove the food at the table, chances are at least one person will send food flying across to the lady in the white dress. At a cocktail party, there are people who fiddle with the skewers or who stab themselves when trying to stuff them in a pocket. Others hold them demurely behind their back, causing irreparable damage to the lady behind. Make sure you provide a bowl for the empty skewers (with a used skewer already in place to demonstrate its purpose) or have someone follow the guests around, removing all weapons.

Karen Miller

ENTERTAINING THOUGHTS

Entertaining is about more than just food. It is about caring and sharing; about conversation and laughter. When I first started cooking, I tried to impress everyone and consequently spent more time in the kitchen than with my guests. Now I know time is precious, and whether it is a more formal setting or something casual, I care more about spending time with my guests than what will actually get to the table (but don't get me wrong, they get well-fed!).

The large part of entertaining well is confidence. As long as you appear relaxed, your guests will probably feel right at home and bring to the table the spirit you want. How to get to that place where cooking dinner for 12 is effortless? For some it comes naturally. Others need practice and for still others it just won't happen—the fear of entertaining is too great to overcome. Start with the level where you are comfortable; if you are at ease your guests will have a better time. Rest assured that everyone will appreciate your efforts. Those who entertain understand the care and attention you put into it; those who don't entertain may have an even greater appreciation of what is involved in preparing and serving food to guests—that may well be why they don't do it themselves!

Practically speaking, the most important thing you can do is be prepared. Plan all the details, organize ("mise en place" is the technical term) and prepare as much as you can ahead of time. I often use my guests as guinea pigs, but most people are more comfortable serving the tried and true. Finally, it's essential to love what you are doing. For me there is something totally satisfying in starting with the best ingredients I can and feeding people, both their stomachs and their souls. Whatever you do, do not give up!

KAREN MILLER

ACCOMPANIMENTS

A LITTLE ON THE SIDE

Roasted Garlic & Cheese Soufflé

Soufflés are one of the mysteries of the sacred sect of "egg cookery," as old-time food writers used to classify it. But they aren't so difficult, and are no great mystery either. They do require a little thought and care, though. Savoury soufflés are made by folding some of the whisked whites into a thick white sauce enriched with yolks. (Use fewer yolks than whites, for added height and lift.) Grated cheeses, meat or vegetable purées and herbs are added for flavour, then the remaining egg whites are folded in. The old writers were right about one thing—a soufflé waits for no one. Have your guests seated and waiting, glasses of wine in hand.

DEE HOBSBAWN-SMITH   SERVES 8 TO 14, DEPENDING ON RAMEKIN SIZE

RECOMMENDED WINE:
Canadian, Alsatian or Italian pinot gris

THE SCIENCE OF SOUFFLÉS

The word "soufflé" comes from the French verb meaning "to blow, to whisper, to breathe," all of which reinforce the notion of fragility. Opening the oven door (changing the air pressure and temperature) can collapse a soufflé in the process of rising. Carrying a soufflé to the table will allow the trapped air and steam to cool and shrink, and poof! it collapses. Bake soufflés at a temperature high enough to set and stabilize the proteins before the foam reaches maximum expansion in the oven, and low enough to heat the interior without burning the exterior. A setting of 400°F (200°C) produces a creamy centre and crusty outside; 325°F (165°C) bakes into a uniformly solid dish with less volume.

DEE HOBSBAWN-SMITH

	butter, for ramekins	
3 Tbsp.	unsalted butter	45 mL
1/2	leek, minced	1/2
1	onion, minced	1
2	bulbs roasted garlic	2
4 Tbsp.	all-purpose flour	60 mL
1/2 cup	dry white wine	120 mL
2 cups	milk	480 mL
6	eggs, separated	6
1 cup	grated Fontina cheese	240 mL
1 cup	grated sharp Cheddar cheese	240 mL
2 Tbsp.	minced fresh chives	30 mL
2 Tbsp.	minced fresh thyme	30 mL
1 tsp.	minced fresh rosemary	5 mL
	freshly ground black pepper to taste	
3/4 tsp.	cream of tartar	4 mL

Preheat the oven to 400°F (200°C). Butter the insides of the ramekins (use a 6- to 8-oz./170- to 225-mL size).

Melt the butter in a heavy sauté pan over medium heat, then add the leek and onion. Cook until the onion is transparent and tender, then add the cloves from the roasted garlic. Stir well. Add the flour and cook for another 2 minutes, until it is light gold and the texture of sand. Stir in the wine, mixing well. Heat the milk in a separate pot, then add it in small increments, stirring well to

prevent lumping. Bring the mixture to a boil, then remove from the heat and add $\frac{1}{2}$ cup (120 mL) of the hot sauce to the egg yolks, stirring briskly. Stir the warmed egg yolks into the sauce. Add the cheeses, herbs and pepper and mix well.

In a clean glass or stainless steel bowl, whisk the egg whites until frothy, then add the cream of tartar. Beat to firm peaks. Lighten the texture of the egg yolk and cheese mixture by folding $\frac{1}{4}$ of the egg whites into the mixture, then fold in the remaining egg whites. Do not overmix.

Gently spoon the mixture into the ramekins, filling each about $\frac{3}{4}$ full. Transfer to a baking sheet and bake on the centre rack of the oven for about 20 minutes, until puffed but not completely set. Serve immediately.

Truffled Couscous

Sous-chef Rogelio Herrara and I conceived this recipe for the 2001 Sterling Silver All-Canadian Chef's Race. It was part of a plate that beat out 4 other chef teams from across Canada. When Rogelio suggested adding coconut to the couscous, I was skeptical. But he was right on—it is a delicious combo.

GAIL NORTON

SERVES 4 TO 6

For the couscous:

2 cups	stock of your choice	480 mL
¼ cup	coconut milk	60 mL
2–5 Tbsp.	olive oil	30–75 mL
2 Tbsp.	butter	30 mL
1	small onion, minced	1
1	clove garlic, minced	1
1	large portobello mushroom, chopped	1
2 Tbsp.	truffle oil	30 mL
2 Tbsp.	truffle paste	30 mL
	salt to taste	
2 cups	couscous	480 mL

Combine the stock and coconut milk in a saucepan and heat to boiling.

Heat about 2 Tbsp. (30 mL) of the olive oil and the butter in a pan and sauté the onion and garlic on high heat for about 2 minutes. Turn down the heat and add the chopped portobello and 1 Tbsp. (15 mL) of the truffle oil. Continue cooking until the mixture is very soft and fragrant. Add the truffle paste and a sprinkle of salt. Taste the mixture—it should have a distinct truffle flavour. Add more paste if necessary.

Add the couscous to the mixture, along with the remaining 1 Tbsp. (15 mL) truffle oil. Then add the boiling stock and coconut milk mixture. Remove from the heat and place a lid on the pan.

For the cream topping:

2 Tbsp.	Devon cream	30 mL
1 Tbsp.	coconut milk	15 mL
	salt to taste	

Whisk together the cream topping ingredients.

To serve:

Top each portion of couscous with a dollop of the cream topping.

Maple-Roasted Butternut Squash

My favourite squash with a touch of maple—there's nothing more to say.

Judy Wood

Serves 6

2 lbs.	butternut squash	900 g
4 Tbsp.	butter	60 mL
2 Tbsp.	brown sugar	30 mL
2 Tbsp.	maple syrup	30 mL
$\frac{1}{2}$ tsp.	salt	2.5 mL
1 Tbsp.	fresh thyme	15 mL

Preheat the oven to 400°F (200°C).

Peel the squash, cut it in half and discard the seeds. Cut the squash into $\frac{1}{3}$-inch-thick (.85-cm) slices and set it aside.

Melt the butter in a small roasting pan on the stovetop. Add the sugar and maple syrup. Cook and stir over low heat for about 2 minutes. Add the salt and squash. Stir until all the squash has been well coated. Place the pan in the oven and bake for about 25 minutes, or until the squash is tender. Remove from the oven, add the thyme and return to the oven for another 5 minutes.

Braised FENNEL with ROSEMARY
Honey & BALSAMIC Vinegar

This is a great side vegetable for a variety of dishes, but fennel always seems to me to be a truly Italian food. Rosemary honey (or any honey, unusual or not; try whatever type strikes your fancy) can be found quite readily in specialty food stores. The addition of dried fennel seeds is optional, but it is an excellent reiteration of flavour for extra punch.

Serves 4   Rhondda Siebens

2 Tbsp.	butter	30 mL
1 Tbsp.	olive oil	15 mL
4	fennel bulbs, trimmed and cut into wedges	4
2	fresh sage leaves	2
	salt and freshly ground black pepper to taste	
1 tsp.	dried fennel seeds (optional)	5 mL
¼ cup	balsamic vinegar	60 mL
3 Tbsp.	rosemary honey	45 mL

Melt the butter and oil in a large heavy pan over medium heat. Add the fennel wedges and sage, turning after a few minutes to coat the pieces and cook on both sides. After approximately 10 minutes, season with salt and pepper. Add the fennel seeds, if using.

Reduce the heat to a simmer and add the balsamic vinegar, turning the fennel to coat it on all sides. Add the honey, cover the pan and cook on low for approximately 20 minutes, stirring occasionally. Add a bit of water, stir the sauce and cook for another 5 to 10 minutes. Check for seasoning and serve immediately.

Roasted Tomato-Stuffed Peppers

This is one of those dishes that I have to make every year when the markets are loaded with peppers and tomatoes. Of course you can use red peppers and red tomatoes, but I like to alternate; yellow peppers with red tomatoes and red peppers with yellow tomatoes. Please don't omit the anchovies even if they are not your favourite. They somehow "melt" into the peppers, adding to the wonderful flavour without being identifiable as anchovies.

RECOMMENDED WINE: full-bodied Rosé from the south of France or lighter tempranillo from Spain

PAM FORTIER

SERVES 6

3	bell peppers, red, orange or yellow (choose peppers that are round rather than long)	3
4	medium-ripe tomatoes, red or yellow, cored and quartered	4
4	cloves garlic, peeled and thinly sliced	4
4	anchovies, packed in oil	4
½ cup	extra virgin olive oil	120 mL
	freshly ground black pepper to taste	

Preheat the oven to 350°F (175°C). Wash the peppers and split them in half from top to bottom. Each half should retain its part of the stem, as this helps the peppers keep their shape. With a small sharp knife, slice through the inner white membrane just under the stem. Remove the membranes and seeds.

Place the peppers in a shallow roasting dish just large enough to hold them. Pack each pepper with the tomatoes, arranging them to fit snugly, skin side up. Divide the garlic slices between the peppers, tucking them here and there between the tomatoes. Break up the anchovies into small pieces and do the same with them. Drizzle with the olive oil, dividing it evenly between the six halves. Bake for approximately 1 hour. These can be eaten right away or kept at room temperature for a couple of hours.

Gilded BRUSSELS SPROUTS

Pity the Brussels sprout. It makes an annual appearance, usually
for the winter festive season, and is then summarily ignored or
dismissed as being "too cabbagey." Like its other cabbage
cousins, this mini head loves the company of pork and is reduced
to sulphurous fumes if overcooked. Dress up your Brussels
sprouts, or use that full-size cabbage you have hidden in the back
of your vegetable bin. For a whole-meal deal, add a generous
amount of thinly sliced potatoes. And never, never apologize!

SERVES 6 TO 8 AS A SIDE DISH   DEE HOBSBAWN-SMITH

2.2 lbs.	Brussels sprouts	1 kg
1 Tbsp.	sunflower oil	15 mL
1	onion, finely diced	1
4–6	cloves garlic, minced	4–6
½ cup	diced ham	120 mL
1 Tbsp.	minced fresh thyme	15 mL
2 cups	whipping cream	480 mL
	salt and freshly ground black pepper to taste	
½ cup	bread crumbs	120 mL
½ cup	grated Parmesan cheese	120 mL
2 Tbsp.	melted butter	30 mL

Preheat the oven to 375°F (190°C). Trim off the ends of the
Brussels sprouts, then thinly slice them. Fill a large shallow sauté
pan with water to a depth of 1 to 2 inches (2.5 to 5 cm) and bring
the water to a rolling boil. Add salt, then add a couple handfuls
of sliced sprouts. Cook over high heat for just a minute or so,
until they turn bright green. Scoop out the sprouts with a slotted
spoon, drain well, then add successive batches until all the
sprouts are blanched. (Cooking them in batches is the easiest
way to prevent overcooking.)

Transfer the sprouts to a gratin dish on a baking sheet (to catch
drips). Dump out the water from the sauté pan, then reheat the
pan. Add the oil, then the onion, garlic and ham. Cook over
medium heat until the onions are tender, about 5 minutes, adding
small amounts of water as needed to prevent browning. Stir the
mixture into the Brussels sprouts, along with the thyme, cream,
salt and pepper. Stir the bread crumbs, cheese and melted
butter together, then sprinkle the crumbs on the gratin. Bake for
30-45 minutes, until the cream is thick and bubbly and the crumbs
are well-browned. Serve hot.

SPINACH WITH MUSTARD SEED

Kissing cousin to the boiled spinach that pleases my Brit friend Sarah, this purée is seasoned with the spices of India. Serve it on a buffet, with an Indian feast or with any pork dish.

DEE HOBSBAWN-SMITH   SERVES 4

1 Tbsp.	sunflower oil	15 mL
1	large onion, chopped	1
6	cloves garlic, minced	6
2 Tbsp.	grated fresh ginger	30 mL
1 Tbsp.	yellow mustard seed	15 mL
2 tsp.	curry powder	10 mL
$\frac{1}{2}$ tsp.	cumin seed	2.5 mL
$\frac{1}{2}$ cup	whipping cream or coconut milk	120 mL
2	bunches spinach	2
1	bunch cilantro	1
	salt and freshly ground black pepper to taste	
1 Tbsp.	lemon juice	15 mL

Heat the oil in a sauté pan, then add the onion, garlic and ginger. Cook for 5 to 7 minutes over medium-high heat, adding small amounts of water as needed to prevent the onion from colouring. When the onion is tender, add the mustard seed, curry powder and cumin seed. Cook for 1 to 2 minutes, until the spices are fragrant. Add the cream or coconut milk, bring to a boil and carefully transfer the mixture to a food processor. Purée to a fine paste, scraping the bowl down once or twice as needed.

Wash the spinach and discard all the stems. Do not dry the leaves. Reheat the pan used for the onions, and place the spinach in the hot pan. Cook it briefly until it wilts, turning the leaves so that they all contact the pan. Drain off any water. Add the spinach to the food processor and purée. Add the salt, pepper and lemon juice. Serve hot.

Herbed White Beans

This dish is a great accompaniment to a lot of things—lamb and pork come instantly to mind. Make it with cannellini or navy beans if that is all that is available. But this salad looks unusual and tastes wonderful made with Emergo beans if you can find them in gourmet shops.

Serves 4   Pam Fortier

2 cups	dried white beans, preferably emergo	480 mL
1	medium cooking onion, peeled and cut in half	1
6	cloves garlic	6
2	bay leaves	2
2	sprigs savoury	2
½ cup	finely chopped red onion	120 mL
½ cup	extra virgin olive oil	120 mL
	salt and freshly ground black pepper to taste	

Place the beans in a bowl large enough to hold 8 cups (2 L). Cover with water and let soak overnight.

To cook, drain the soaking liquid from the beans. Place the beans in a medium pot and cover with water by an inch or two (2.5 to 5 cm). Add the cooking onion, unpeeled garlic, bay leaves and savoury to the pot. Bring to a boil over high heat. Lower the heat, partially cover the beans and simmer for 45 minutes to 1 hour, or until a tested bean is tender.

Drain the beans, discard the aromatics and place the beans in a bowl. While still warm, add the chopped red onion and olive oil. Stir to combine. Season with salt and pepper. Serve at room temperature.

FENNEL SLAW

I fell in love with fennel a couple of years ago and find it goes especially well with grilled shrimp or roast pork. My dog even loves it! This is a fresh-tasting side dish that's easy to prepare and serve.

PAM FORTIER

SERVES 4

1	large bulb fennel	1
1 tsp.	Dijon mustard	5 mL
3 tsp.	Ricard or Pernod	15 mL
1 Tbsp.	sherry vinegar	15 mL
3 Tbsp.	extra virgin olive oil	45 mL
1	shallot, peeled and finely minced	1
	salt and freshly ground black pepper to taste	

Remove or trim the outer leaves of the fennel. Break the bulb into separate leaves and wash. Slice into matchstick pieces and place in a bowl.

In a small bowl, combine the mustard, Ricard or Pernod and sherry vinegar. Whisk in the olive oil. Stir in the shallot. Toss with the fennel and season with salt and pepper. Allow to marinate a couple of hours at room temperature before serving.

HOW TO SAVE A DISH FROM OVER-SALTING

Over-salting is something that happens to every cook from time to time. I had one disastrous dinner where I had added so much sea salt to the risotto that it was inedible (picture guests downing jugs of water). After trying many obscure home remedies, such as adding tomatoes, the consensus seemed to be that sugar is the magic ingredient to correct over-salting mistakes. It's a matter of rebalancing the flavours. If all else fails, however, you can always order in a pizza!

RHONDDA SIEBENS

FEEDING THE SENSES

When I entertain I like to engage the senses. I usually have some part of the meal cooking or baking when guests arrive; they are drawn in by the aroma and appetites are piqued. Soft lighting and flickering candles create a warm atmosphere. A good conversation grouping, whether it be around a kitchen island or in the living room, gets people face to face and interacting.

Pre-selected and loaded music means I won't have to go rummaging around for a certain CD. Mellow jazz is my favourite for a dinner party, especially the old standards. Verve Records has a series called "Jazz 'Round Midnight" that features beautiful piano or saxophone compilations.

People relax and feel pampered when their favourite cocktail arrives quickly. Things may go wrong, but with a drink in hand, most people will sit back and enjoy the show. There should also be something salty to nibble on. Having something to eat for those who are "starving" allows them to relax and enjoy the pacing of the evening. I usually opt for olives and cheese, with crackers or baguette.

Because I don't have a kitchen geared to entertaining, I like to have most of the dinner pre-organized. In cooler weather that means on the stove, with another hour or two of simmering. In summer, the meat is pre-marinated or I have seafood that is quick to grill. That way I can relax and spend more time with my guests.

It is fun sometimes to present plated food, but I find it creates a relaxed atmosphere when dinner is served "family-style." I like to put the entire main course on a large platter in the centre of the table. The centrepiece might be char-grilled lamb chops nestled on a bed of cheesy pasta, surrounded by glistening grilled vegetables, with basil sprigs tucked here and there for extra colour. Everybody gets into the spirit, helping themselves to exactly as much as they want, and no one has to stand on formality, waiting to be asked if they want seconds.

PAM FORTIER

186

An Entertaining Change of Life

After years of engineering food, fun and parties for other people, my personal preferences for entertaining have changed.

For well over a decade, I fed people countless little bites at the parties my company catered, and from the kitchen of my restaurant. At home, I regularly fed friends and colleagues, filling the house and my table on week nights and holidays. I pressed everyone I could into KP duty and consciously chose dishes that could be made in advance, leaving me ostensibly free to enjoy my own party.

Never happened.

Somehow, even in my own home, I felt like a caterer. I never quite made it to those heart-to-heart conversations I had hoped to create. I was too busy managing the day. It was time to change how I did things.

It was a red-letter day, after years of stubbornly doing it myself, when I had my first potluck on my patio table. That evening, I learned to have faith in the golden rule of potlucks: people bring their favourite dish, and magically, the unplanned menu harmonizes without overlap. The kitchen goddess will organize things if you just let go and let her!

At the other end of the spectrum, I have adopted the intimate "dinner for four" as an ideal way to entertain. It means that my friends can congregate close by, leaning on the counter to chat while I finish up the last-minute bits. I prefer to set out simple food that won't absorb me to the exclusion of my guests; we eat burgers or curried lamb shoulder, or my current salad-pasta combo. I don't need to indulge in high-wire culinary pyrotechnics anymore; I just want to feed my friends and hang out with them. And I hate constructing hors d'oeuvre! I am more likely to set out a bowl of good olives or caramelized nuts to stave off starvation until dinner is ready.

My entertaining style has changed partly because my pragmatic nature has bowed to the inevitable: in my tiny home, there is simply no room for a table that seats 12, or for a lot of people to gather in my galley kitchen. It does mean that I can pay attention to the people who matter in my life, instead of getting swept up, lost in a crowd in my own home. I still, however, like to plate things while everyone waits, glass of wine in hand. There's nothing amiss in a little bit of drama!

DEE HOBSBAWN-SMITH

187

Entertaining in Point Form

I am a chef first and foremost and 98 percent of the writing I have done over the last 20 years has been in list or in point form. That style of thought contributes greatly to my no-nonsense, get-the-job-done, be-organized approach to home entertaining. My most frequently asked question is, "Do you cook at home?" The answer is most definitely, yes! And I enjoy it! Entertaining represents a desire to give and share with others, and it has to come from the heart first.

To be a great entertainer or chef, you have to really love to do it, really want to do it. Having said that, let me share (in point form, of course) some of the things I keep in mind when planning to entertain guests in my home.

• Keep ingredients and flavours familiar; it's okay to mix them up, but just try to stay away from the wildly exotic.

• Have some nibbles out when guests arrive.

• Allow guests to wear their shoes.

• Try to have much of the preparation done beforehand so you can spend time visiting with your guests (unless the guests are sous-chefs!).

• Pay attention to little details that make for an overall big impact: candles, floral arrangements, music selection and lighting all help create magic.

• Have a clean house or, at the very least, clean bathrooms.

• Unless you know for sure that all your guests will enjoy your dog, send it outside, downstairs or to the movies.

• When appropriate, get guests involved: have them participate in making drinks, selecting music, setting the table or stuffing the ravioli.

• Offer beverages other than alcohol, and have a good supply of bottled or filtered water.

• When choosing the menu, less is often more. Try not to overdo plates with sauces and garnishes.

• Pick high-quality ingredients at the peak of seasonal freshness.

• Serve recipes you are familiar with, so you know they work and you are comfortable with them.

• If possible, hire staff. Chefs have help, why not you? If someone clears, pours wine and does dishes, you will have more time to spend with your guests and they will have a better time.

• Try serving dessert away from the table, in another room or outside if weather allows.

• Serve decaffeinated coffee.

• Turn off the ringer on your phone, pager and cell phone.

• Clean up tomorrow.

SHELLEY ROBINSON

ENDINGS

BAKING & SWEETS

CRUNCHY CRANBERRY BANANA MUFFINS

Very popular with kids and adults at Caffè Beano, this muffin descends from a sugarless muffin that I used to make in the back-country in my former health food days. It still retains the healthy use of banana as the primary sweetener with the millet as the secret ingredient that makes the crunchy texture. If this is too many muffins for your purposes, you can halve the recipe.

MAKES 4 DOZEN

RHONDDA SIEBENS

4 cups	ripe, mashed banana (about 7 or 8 bananas)	950 mL
3	eggs	3
1½ cups	sugar	360 mL
4¼ cups	buttermilk	1 L
1 cup	millet	240 mL
¾ cup	bran	180 mL
1 tsp.	ground cinnamon	5 mL
2 Tbsp.	baking soda	30 mL
1 Tbsp.	salt	15 mL
1 cup	water	240 mL
½ lb.	butter, melted (or 1 cup/240 mL canola oil)	225 g
8 cups	all-purpose flour	2 L
1½ cups	bran	360 mL
4¼ cups	fresh cranberries	1 L

Mash the banana and set aside. Cream the eggs and sugar together in a large bowl. Mix in the mashed banana. Add the buttermilk and stir.

In a separate bowl, combine the millet, ¾ cup (180 mL) bran, cinnamon, baking soda and salt. Mix well. Combine the water with the butter or oil and add it to the millet mixture, mixing well. Add this wet mixture to the banana-buttermilk mixture and stir well to combine.

In a separate bowl, combine the flour, bran and cranberries. Add in 2 or 3 stages to the wet ingredients, folding it in and being careful not to overstir.

Preheat the oven to 325°F (165°C). Grease four 12-cup muffin tins. Fill the prepared tins with the batter. Bake for approximately 25 minutes, until golden brown.

Bartlett Pears Poached in Saffron Star Anise
& Black Peppercorn Sauternes (p. 212)

My Mother's Shortbread Cookies (p. 193), Brown Sugar Pecan
Cookies (p. 196) and Chocolate & Cherry Mosaic Biscotti (p. 197)

Fresh-Shucked Oysters with a Demi-sec Vouvray Vinaigrette Drizzle
(p. 40), Spinach, Lemon & Thyme Soup (p. 84), My Favourite
Asparagus Salad (p. 92), Herb-Crusted Lamb Chops with Olive Aïoli
(p. 118) and Tarte au Fromage Blanc (p. 223)

Brie in Silk Pyjamas with
Brioche Crostini (p. 228)

My Mother's Shortbread Cookies

If my mother is famous for anything, it is this recipe. I can tell you she is not famous for the actual transcription of any recipe as they generally contain only a list of ingredients (not necessarily including quantities) and no instructions. Those are all in her head. Anyone tasting these melt-in-your-mouth morsels always asks what the secret ingredient is. There is none. But you do have to follow simple rules. Start with soft salted butter, stir by hand and do it with love and patience (my mother knows not of unsalted butter, Kitchen Aid mixers or convection ovens). Make these all year round. They will keep in a tightly sealed container for 4 to 5 days, but they rarely last that long.

MAKES 25 TO 30 COOKIES   KAREN MILLER

½ cup	cornstarch	120 mL
½ cup	icing sugar	120 mL
1 cup	salted butter, softened	240 mL
1 cup	flour	240 mL

Preheat the oven to 300°F (150°C). Mix the ingredients together by hand gently until the flour is incorporated. Form 1 Tbsp. (15 mL) of dough into a ball and place on a baking sheet, spacing the balls about 2 inches (5 cm) apart. Do not overwork the dough at this stage, and if the dough gets too soft, put it in the refrigerator for a while. Press down on the ball with a wet fork to flatten slightly. Bake for about 20 minutes. Do not let the cookies brown. Remove from the oven and cool on the pan. Do not try to remove the cookies from the pan until cool.

Caramel Pecan Banana Pumpkin Muffins

Everything in this recipe is the best—caramel, pecans, banana, pumpkin—so how can these muffins not be the best? Try them yourself. Use homemade caramel sauce if you can, but the store-bought canned variety works fine.

Karen Miller

MAKES 12 muffins

3/4 cup	pecans, roughly chopped	180 mL
1/2 cup	Caramel Sauce	120 mL
2 cups	flour	480 mL
1 Tbsp.	baking powder	15 mL
1/2 tsp.	salt	2.5 mL
1 tsp.	ground cinnamon	5 mL
1 cup	milk	240 mL
2	eggs	2
2/3 cup	butter, melted	160 mL
1/2 cup	mashed ripe banana	120 mL
1/2 cup	pumpkin purée	120 mL
1/2 cup	sugar	120 mL

Preheat the oven to 375°F (190°C). Line a 12-cup muffin pan with paper cups. Combine the pecans and Caramel Sauce on a baking sheet and bake until bubbly, about 15 minutes. Let cool.

Combine the flour, baking powder, salt and cinnamon in a large bowl. Mix the milk, eggs and melted butter in a separate bowl and add to the flour mixture. Stir the batter only to combine. Stir in the mashed banana and pumpkin purée, and then the sugar. Add the pecan/caramel mixture. Spoon the batter into the prepared muffin tin. Bake until golden brown on top, about 18 minutes.

Homemade Pumpkin Purée

I buy sugar pie pumpkins at the farmers' market in the fall, bake them and purée the sweet flesh to freeze for winter risotto and other baked goods. Do not use ordinary carving pumpkins—the flesh will be too watery. Cut the pumpkins in half and remove the seeds and membranes. Place cut side up in a baking pan, cover with foil and bake at 350°F (175°C) until tender, about 40 to 50 minutes, depending on the size. Let cool, remove the skin and purée in a blender or food processor.

Karen Miller

Caramel Sauce

1½ cups	sugar	360 mL
½ cup	water	120 mL
1 cup	whipping cream	240 mL

Stir the water and sugar together in a saucepan. Place over medium heat and cook, without stirring, until the mixture turns a golden amber colour. Remove from the heat and add the cream carefully—it will bubble up. Stir until smooth. Use immediately or let cool and refrigerate for up to 5 days.

BROWN SUGAR PECAN COOKIES

Buttery, butterscotchy, nutty, mmmmm, . . . Adapted from *Gourmet's Best Desserts*, published by the editors of *Gourmet* magazine.

PAM FORTIER

MAKES ABOUT 30 COOKIES

1 cup	pecans	240 mL
1 cup	unsalted butter, room temperature	240 mL
1 cup	brown sugar	240 mL
2 cups	all-purpose flour	480 mL

Preheat the oven to 350°F (175°C). Toast the pecans until fragrant, approximately 7 to 8 minutes. Cool. In a food processor, process until finely ground.

Cream the butter in a mixer with a paddle attachment. Add the sugar and continue creaming. Scrape down the bowl, mix again and add the flour. When just mixed, add the pecans and combine. The mixture may appear dry and crumbly at this point. Use a small ice cream scoop (or tablespoon) to shape into balls, squeezing together to hold shape if necessary. Flatten onto a parchment-lined baking sheet. Bake for approximately 6 to 8 minutes, or until the edges are starting to become golden brown.

CHOCOLATE & CHERRY MOSAIC BISCOTTI

This began life as a sweet Italian dough that I used endlessly for fruit tarts. But it was so good alone that it gradually morphed into a cookie, first as a rolled or dropped version, then a log that was double-baked in the biscotti style.

MAKES ABOUT 30 COOKIES   DEE HOBSBAWN-SMITH

2 cups	all-purpose flour	480 mL
2 cups	icing sugar	480 mL
1/2 cup	cold unsalted butter	120 mL
1	egg	1
1	egg yolk	1
1 tsp.	vanilla extract	5 mL
2 Tbsp.	milk	30 mL
2 Tbsp.	finely grated fresh ginger	30 mL
1/2 cup	almonds	120 mL
1/2 cup	chopped semi-sweet chocolate	120 mL
1/2 cup	chopped dried sour cherries	120 mL
1/2 cup	chopped dried Bing cherries	120 mL

Preheat the oven to 350°F (175°C). Combine the flour and icing sugar. Blend together the butter, egg, egg yolk, vanilla, milk and ginger. Add to the flour and sugar, blending well, then add the remaining ingredients. Form into 2 logs about 2 inches (5 cm) in diameter. Line 2 baking sheets with parchment paper and place the logs on the sheets. Bake for about 30 minutes. Allow to cool on the sheets, then slice on the diagonal into 1/2-inch (1.2-cm) fingers. Arrange on the baking sheet, cut side up, and bake another 15 minutes, or until completely dry. Cool on the baking sheets. Store in a glass jar or tin when cool.

KILO CAKE

Not for lightweights, this cake delivers the goods—an entire kilo-gram of semi-sweet chocolate forms the basis of what is a serious chocoholic's indulgence. But because of its richness and the fact that it serves so many, it does provide a good return for the rela-tively small time invested! As with anything of value, this dessert is only as good as its ingredients, so buy the best. I like to use Callebaut . . . It might help to think of it as a kilo of gold instead.

DEE HOBSBAWN-SMITH   SERVES 16

2.2 lbs.	semi-sweet Callebaut chocolate, finely chopped	1 kg
1 lb.	unsalted butter	450 g
8	eggs, at room temperature	8
½ cup	double espresso, slightly cooled	120 mL
1 Tbsp.	ground espresso	15 mL
⅓ cup	all-purpose flour	80 mL
1 recipe	Dark Chocolate Ganache	1 recipe
½ cup	toasted sliced almonds	120 mL

Butter and flour a 10-inch (25-cm) springform pan. Tear off a sheet of foil that is about 4 inches (10 cm) longer than the circumference of the pan. Fold it in half lengthwise and use the doubled length as a collar around the outside of the springform, folding the foil over itself to secure it where the ends meet.

Preheat the oven to 325°F (165°C). Place the oven rack in the lowest position.

Melt the chocolate and butter at medium heat for about 4 minutes in the microwave, stirring after 2 minutes and again when melted.

Using a mixer, beat the eggs on high speed with a whisk attach-ment for about 7 minutes, or until the eggs triple in volume and are pale in colour. Use a rubber spatula to fold the eggs into the chocolate-butter mixture, adding the espresso, ground espresso and flour before the mixture is completely incorporated. Stir only enough to blend.

Gently transfer the batter into the prepared springform pan, working close to the base of the pan to prevent deflating the batter. Slide the cake into the oven and bake for 45 minutes.

Cool the cake for 5 minutes on a wire rack, then gently remove the foil collar. Use a small, thin-bladed, sharp knife to loosen the cake from the sides of the springform. Leave the cake in the pan until it is completely cool and well-chilled, then remove the sides of the springform. Leave the cake on the springform base. Glaze the cake, using the inside of a tablespoon to spread the ganache over the curve of the cake's upper surface. Sprinkle the almonds along the upper crust around the outer rim.

Slice this cake with a thin-bladed knife dipped in hot water, and use a firm downward pressure. It is very dense, and sawing will ruin its lines. Use a pointed cake lifter to lift each slice from the springform base.

Dark Chocolate Ganache

MAKES ABOUT 1 CUP (240 ML)

½ cup	whipping cream	120 mL
6 oz.	semi-sweet chocolate, chopped	180 g
1 Tbsp.	orange or coffee liqueur	15 mL

Heat the cream to just below a boil and let it cool slightly. Melt the chocolate at medium heat for 2 to 3 minutes in the microwave, stirring once or twice. Add the warm cream and the liqueur to the chocolate, stir well and cool slightly before using as a glaze.

LEMON POPPY SEED CHIFFON
CAKE WITH LEMON VODKA GLAZE

I love lemon, especially with poppy seeds. It wins over chocolate anytime, no contest! Chiffon cake wins too, for its lovely moist texture and its goofproof low-fat nature. This makes a handsome tall cake when it is baked in a tube or bundt pan, but for cutesy-woo individual cakelets, bake the batter in ramekins or immaculate ungreased muffin cups. Avoid overbaking at all cost!

DEE HOBSBAWN-SMITH   SERVES 14

2¼ cups	cake flour	540 mL
3 Tbsp.	poppy seeds	45 mL
1½ cups	sugar	360 mL
½ tsp.	baking soda	2.5 mL
½ tsp.	salt	2.5 mL
½ cup	sunflower or safflower oil	120 mL
⅔ cup	orange juice	160 mL
2 Tbsp.	lemon juice	30 mL
1 Tbsp.	finely grated lemon zest	15 mL
1 tsp.	vanilla extract	5 mL
7	large eggs, separated	7
3	additional egg whites	3
1¼ tsp.	cream of tartar	6.2 mL
1 recipe	Lemon Vodka Glaze (optional)	1 recipe

Preheat the oven to 325°F (165°C) and set the rack at its lowest position.

Combine the flour, poppy seeds, sugar, baking soda and salt in a large bowl, reserving 2 Tbsp. (30 mL) of the sugar. Mix well. Make a well in the centre and add the oil, orange juice, lemon juice, lemon zest, vanilla and egg yolks. Beat for 1 minute, or until smooth.

In a separate bowl, whisk all the egg whites until frothy. Add the cream of tartar and reserved 2 Tbsp. (30 mL) sugar; beat to the soft peak stage. Fold the whites into the batter until just blended.

Pour into an ungreased tube pan and bake for 55 minutes. Invert the pan for about 2 hours to cool. Loosen with a knife or spatula, remove from the pan and drizzle with glaze if you wish. Serve in wedges.

Lemon Vodka Glaze

2 cups	icing sugar	480 mL
1 tsp.	finely grated lemon zest (optional)	5 mL
	lemon-infused vodka as needed	

Combine the icing sugar and the zest, then slowly add the vodka by the teaspoon, mixing well, until a glazing consistency is achieved.

"Don't Tell" Tiramisu

By now just about everyone has at least heard of tiramisu, and maybe, just maybe, the feverish race for every restaurant to have tiramisu on its dessert menu is over. Perhaps we (lovers of tiramisu) can get down to the business of making it again with pride. Of course, like all things traditional, every Nona (Italian grandma) or descendant thereof has a family recipe. This is one I was specifically asked not to tell, but what the heck, some things in life are just too good not to share. The ingredients are all available at Italian specialty markets. Most towns and certainly all cities have one or more as the Italians have such a rich food culture and so many wonderful products from the homeland.

Shelley Robinson

Serves 12

12	egg yolks	12
1½ cups	sugar	360 mL
1 lb.	mascarpone cheese, room temperature	450 g
2	lemons, zest and juice	2
4 cups	full-strength espresso, or very strong coffee, cold	950 mL
½ cup	amaretto (optional, but really a must)	120 mL
½ cup	Marsala (optional; I usually use a little bit more)	120 mL
48	Italian ladyfinger biscuits	48
½ cup	freshly ground espresso beans	120 mL

In a mixer or with a hand-held beater, blend the egg yolks and sugar on high speed until the mixture is thick and pale. (Hint: it is impossible to overdo this step and beating it well is extremely crucial to the outcome of the texture.) Scrape out ⅔ of this mixture and set it aside in a bowl. Add the mascarpone to the remaining ⅓ mixture and begin to blend on very low speed, scraping down the sides of the bowl frequently, until the mixture is smooth. Add the lemon juice and zest and blend on low until it is incorporated. Still on low speed, pour the remaining ⅔ egg-sugar mixture slowly down the side of the mixer while it is running, ⅓ at a time. Stop the mixer between each addition and scrape down the sides of the bowl so the whole thing will be one lovely, smooth, creamy, pillowy batter. When the whole mixture has been incorporated on low, crank up the speed to high for 10 seconds—no longer! This will help to further fluff up the batter by incorporating air, but you don't want to add too much or the mixture could break and deflate just like a balloon.

MASCARPONE

This soft, fresh cow's milk cheese has a flavour and texture between cream cheese and butter. It is used in many dessert recipes, as well as being a great (although decadent) addition to savoury sauces. Try mascarpone on fresh baked and toasted bread or French toast.

Shelley Robinson

Spread about 2 Tbsp. (30 mL) of the mixture evenly on the bottom of an 8- x 12- x 3-inch (20- x 30- x 7.5-cm) glass or plastic container. The size of the container is important so that all the ladyfingers will line up and fit together to form the cake.

Combine the coffee with the amaretto and Marsala, if using. Taking two ladyfinger biscuits at a time, dip them into the mixture for about $1\frac{1}{2}$ seconds. Remove and shake off the excess liquid while they are over the bowl of liquid. Quickly place the soaked biscuits into position at the bottom of the container, side by side. You will have 12 up one side and 12 up the other side. Do not oversoak the ladyfingers; if they are too wet, the cake will just slide around and turn to mush, plus you will run out of liquid to soak them in before you finish. If you undersoak the ladyfingers, they will be hard and crunchy, and they won't be the perfect mate to the lush pillow you have just created, so take your time.

When you have 24 perfectly soaked biscuits lining the bottom of the container, use a spatula to spread $\frac{1}{2}$ the remaining egg-cheese mixture over top. Repeat the same process for a second layer. Finish by sprinkling the ground espresso over top. Chill for at least 2 hours before serving. Each portion should have 4 biscuits. Enjoy, and please don't tell anyone where you got this recipe!

CRÈME BRÛLÉE WITH PUMPKIN ESSENCE

Crème brûlée is one of my favourite desserts, so any derivative is a welcome way to enjoy it again and again. The addition of pumpkin makes it an alternative for Thanksgiving dinner in lieu of pumpkin pie. Try making this in larger dishes, which creates a flatter and more shallow crème with more of the caramelized sugar (one of the best parts!).

RHONDDA SIEBENS   SERVES 6

2 cups	whipping cream	480 mL
2/3 cup	whole milk	160 mL
1/4 cup	granulated sugar	60 mL
2	eggs	2
3	egg yolks	3
1/2 tsp.	vanilla extract	2.5 mL
1/2 cup	pumpkin purée	120 mL
3/4 cup	light brown sugar	180 mL

Preheat the oven to 325°F (165°C). Place the cream, milk and sugar in a double boiler or a heavy saucepan and heat to almost boiling.

Beat the eggs and yolks together in a bowl. Whisk the cream mixture into the eggs, beating constantly, then return to the double boiler to cook over medium heat for a few minutes. Stir in the vanilla extract and fold in the pumpkin so that it ribbons through the mixture.

Pour the custard into 6 ramekins. Place them in a large pan and pour enough hot water into the outer pan so that it comes halfway up the sides of the ramekins. Bake for approximately 45 minutes, until the custard is set. Cool to room temperature, then cover and chill, preferably overnight.

Before serving, sprinkle the brown sugar evenly over the custards. Caramelize with a torch or place under a very hot broiler until the sugar caramelizes.

Note: If you're making your own pumpkin purée from sweet, or sugar, pumpkin, be sure to reduce the mixture sufficiently, as it contains a fair amount of water. Alternatively, canned pumpkin purée can be used.

Espresso Pavlova

Australians and New Zealanders debate which country created this tribute to the famous ballerina, but regardless of its origins, it is delicious and festive looking. I love espresso and try my hardest to add it to everything that I make.

SERVES 10   RHONDDA SIEBENS

8	egg whites, at room temperature	8
½ tsp.	salt	2.5 mL
½ tsp.	cream of tartar	2.5 mL
2 cups	fine granulated white sugar	480 mL
2½ Tbsp.	cornstarch	37.5 mL
4 tsp.	vinegar (white or white wine variety)	20 mL
2 tsp.	vanilla extract	10 mL
¼ cup	espresso, at room temperature	60 mL
2 cups	whipping cream	480 mL
4 cups	whole strawberries	950 mL

In a large bowl, beat the egg whites, salt, and cream of tartar together until the whites are very stiff. Slowly add the sugar, beating until stiff. The mixture should be glossy. Beat in the cornstarch, then the vinegar and vanilla extract. At the very end, carefully fold in the espresso so that it ribbons through the mixture.

Preheat the oven to 275°F (135°C). Turn the mixture out onto a large piece of wax paper set on top of a cookie sheet or simply set on the oven rack. The mixture should loosely resemble the shape of a round cake.

Bake for 1 to 1½ hours. The meringue should be golden brown but moist on the inside.

Cool on a rack, then remove the wax paper and place on a large platter. Whip the cream and spread over the meringue. Cover with strawberries.

Chocolate Pâte Spumoni

This easy and elegant dessert has a festive flavour to it that I liken to Christmas cake. Adapt the fruit as your personal preference dictates. Try cutting the slices into bite-size pieces for an after-dessert treat. Look for gold leaf and glacéed fruits at specialty shops.

SHELLEY ROBINSON   SERVES 6 TO 8

½ cup	coarsely chopped pecans	120 mL
½ cup	coarsely chopped unsalted pistachio nuts	120 mL
⅓ cup	coarsely chopped glacé pineapple	80 mL
⅓ cup	coarsely chopped glacé apricots	80 mL
6 oz.	English shortbread biscuits, diced	168 g
6 oz.	dark chocolate, chopped	168 g
⅔ cup	sugar	160 mL
¼ cup	water	60 mL
¾ cup	unsalted butter, softened	180 mL
1 cup	cocoa powder	240 mL
1 Tbsp.	orange liqueur, such as Triple Sec	15 mL
1 tsp.	lemon zest	5 mL
1 tsp.	orange zest	5 mL
1	egg	1
2	egg yolks	2
1	sheet gold leaf, for garnish	1

Oil a 9- x 5- x 3-inch (23- x 12.5- x 7.5-cm) loaf pan, line the bottom and sides with foil and oil the foil. Combine the pecans, pistachios, pineapple, apricots and biscuits in a bowl.

Melt the chocolate in the top of a double boiler over hot water. Boil the sugar and water in a saucepan to melt the sugar and create a syrup; cool. In a large bowl whisk together the butter and cocoa until smooth; add the sugar syrup, melted chocolate, liqueur, lemon and orange zest, egg and egg yolks. Mix the ingredients well to thoroughly combine. Fold in the fruit and nut mixture. Press the mixture into the prepared loaf pan, pressing it well into the corners and making the top level. Cover with plastic wrap and refrigerate for at least 12 hours.

MELTING CHOCOLATE

Chocolate melts in your mouth and melts in your hand. Why? Because it is extremely heat sensitive. When melting chocolate, high heat is not only unnecessary but it can also damage its texture, appearance and taste. There is one basic rule: keep the heat gentle and the chocolate dry. Even a drop of moisture can cause melting chocolate to suddenly stiffen and become unmanageable. The easiest way to melt it is over indirect heat—specifically, a double boiler or bain-marie (water bath). Set a bowl over a pot with about 2 inches (5 cm) of hot but not simmering water. Ensure that the bowl is heatproof (stainless steel) and not touching the water or hanging over the sides where the chocolate could be exposed to direct flame. Be sure to watch that the water does not boil and stir frequently so that all the chocolate comes into contact with the warm bottom. The smaller and more evenly you chop the chocolate, the quicker it will melt.

SHELLEY ROBINSON

To unmould, run a hot knife between the foil and the pan and dip the pan quickly into hot water. Invert onto a serving platter. Carefully remove the foil. To serve, press torn strips of gold leaf onto each slice.

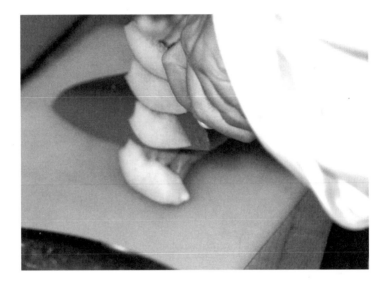

Prairie Fruit Salad
(or Depression Fruit Salad)

Yes, believe it or not, this *is* that seemingly horrible marshmallow salad that your aunt Beatrice always serves at Thanksgiving or Christmas dinner. I happen to love it, and it has been a tradition in my family for years. My grandmother calls it Depression Fruit Salad, explaining that with no fresh produce in the dead of winter, this was the only "salad" that they could muster.

Rhondda Siebens

Serves 6 to 8

1	28-oz. (796-mL) can crushed pineapple	1
1½ lbs.	red seedless grapes, cut in half	680 g
1 lb.	small marshmallows	450 g
	pinch salt	
1	egg	1
1	lemon, juice only	1
1 cup	whipping cream	240 mL

Drain the pineapple, reserving the liquid. Mix the drained pineapple, grapes, marshmallows and pinch of salt in a serving bowl.

Beat the egg, ½ cup (120 mL) of the pineapple juice and the lemon juice together. Cook over medium heat in a small saucepan until the mixture thickens. Set aside to cool.

Add the whipped cream to the cooled mixture and pour it over the grape, marshmallow and pineapple mixture in the bowl. Place in the refrigerator overnight.

Brûléed Apricots
with Amaretti Crumble

This is simple and delicious—but you must wait until the summer season when apricots are perfectly ripe. If you don't like grappa, use brandy or even amaretto for a double shot of almond flavour. Start with the best fresh fruit and you'll have a great dessert.

SERVES 6   CINDA CHAVICH

¼ cup	unsalted butter, melted	60 mL
2 Tbsp.	vanilla extract	30 mL
¼ cup	grappa or brandy	60 mL
¼ cup	smooth apricot preserves	60 mL
12	ripe apricots, washed, halved and pitted	12
½ cup	mascarpone, beaten with a little cream to soften slightly	120 mL
6	crumbled amaretti cookies	6

Preheat the broiler. Combine the melted butter, vanilla, grappa or brandy and apricot preserves. Force the preserves through a sieve if they are not perfectly smooth. Whisk together well.

Arrange the apricots, cut side up, in a 9- x 13-inch (23- x 33-cm) baking dish. Drizzle each apricot with some of the sauce. Place the baking dish on the middle rack, under the hot broiler, for 5 minutes, or until the fruit is just beginning to brown and caramelize.

Arrange 4 apricot halves on each plate, adding a dab of mascarpone to the centre of each fruit. Sprinkle with amaretti cookie crumbs and serve warm (with more grappa and amaretti cookies on the side).

Apples in Wellies

Fruit makes a better "Wellington" than expensive tenderloin—it doesn't mind the steaming that spoils beef while encased in pastry! Choose an apple that won't cook down into mush—Fuji, Mutsu, Granny Smith, Gala, Jonathan, and Cox's Orange Pippin. Once made and stashed in the freezer, the pastry forms the backbone of a number of sweets and savouries. Serve this with either of Pam's ice creams (see pages 215, 217) or with Karen's Caramel Sauce (page 195).

DEE HOBSBAWN-SMITH   SERVES 10

1 recipe	Quick Puff Pastry	1 recipe
10	apples, peeled and cored	10
1	egg, well whisked	1
¼ cup	milk or cream	60 mL
10 Tbsp.	unsalted butter	150 mL
¼ cup	Demerara sugar	60 mL
¼ cup	toasted pine nuts	60 mL
¼ cup	dried cranberries or currants	60 mL
¼ tsp.	ground cinnamon	1.2 mL
¼ tsp.	ground nutmeg	1.2 mL
	granulated sugar for sprinkling	
	ice cream, for garnish	

Roll out ½ of the pastry to ¼ inch (.6 cm) thickness. Cut rounds to cover and fit the whole apples, about 6 to 8 inches (15 to 20 cm), depending on the size of the apples.

Whisk the egg and milk or cream together in a small bowl. This is egg wash, serving as both glue and glaze. Mix together the butter, Demerara sugar, pine nuts, cranberries or currants, cinnamon and nutmeg. Stuff the core cavity of each apple with the filling. Centre each apple on a round of pastry and draw the edges up around the top of the apple. Pinch the edges shut, or overlap the edges and seal them with the egg wash. Use the pastry trimmings to cut out leaves. Place the leaves strategically over any seams, gluing them down with egg wash. Use a sharp paring knife to cut several short slits in the pastry at the top of each apple to allow steam to escape during baking. Chill the pastry-wrapped apples for a minimum of 30 minutes before baking.

Preheat the oven to 425°F (220°C). Brush the entire surface of the pastry with the egg wash. Sprinkle with sugar. Bake the apples on a parchment-lined baking sheet for 20 minutes. Reduce the heat to 375°F (190°C) and bake for another 20 to 30 minutes. Turn the apples several times to ensure even colouration. Cool for a few minutes before serving.

Quick Puff Pastry

Makes 2 lbs. (900 g)

1 lb.	unsalted butter, cold	450 g
4 cups	all-purpose flour	950 g
	salt to taste	
1 cup	ice water	240 mL

Cut the butter into half lengthwise, then turn it and cut it again lengthwise, to make quarters. Slice the quarters into small flat squares. Measure the flour and salt onto the counter and add the butter. Toss together, make a well in the middle, then add the water, stirring with your fingers within the well to blend. Using your hands like forks, with fingers stiffly extended, gently toss the dough up several times, working in the flour and adding more cold water as needed until the dough just holds together. Dust the counter with flour and pat the dough into a rough rectangle. Fold into thirds, brushing off the flour and lining up the edges. Turn the dough 90 degrees so that it is lying length-wise on the counter.

Begin double turns. Roll out the dough into a rectangle about 18 inches (46 cm) long and 6 inches (15 cm) wide, with straight edges and square corners. Bring both short ends into the middle where they should just touch, brush off all the flour, then fold in half so the folded ends meet. (This is called a book fold.) Turn 90 degrees to lie lengthwise, roll out and repeat, then gently mark the dough with two finger indentations to keep track of the number of turns. Cover and chill for 30 minutes. Bring the pastry to the counter and let it sit at room temperature until the dough is pliable enough to fold without cracking the butter. Repeat the book fold twice, chilling between each double turn, for a total of 3 double turns. Mark the dough with finger indentations after each pair of turns.

The dough is now ready to use, with all the layers of butter and dough developed. Store on flour-dusted parchment, loosely covered, in the fridge until needed. After removing from the fridge, let stand on the counter for about 40 minutes before use to soften the butter and prevent cracking. Freeze if the dough is not used up within 4 days.

Bartlett PEARS Poached in SAFFRON Star Anise & BLACK PEPPERCORN Sauternes

This dessert is stunning! It is also incredibly easy to prepare and can be done a day ahead, leaving only the plating for the final day. This makes a good dessert for a heavy meal, as it is light and not too sweet. The saffron gives the pears and the sauce an electric yellow hue, which looks beautiful when served on white plates.

JANET WEBB

SERVES 6

6	firm Bartlett pears	6
1	bottle good-quality Sauternes or other dessert wine	1
1 tsp.	saffron threads	5 mL
6	star anise pods, preferably whole	6
2 tsp.	black peppercorns	10 mL
2 Tbsp.	liquid honey	30 mL
	soft whipped cream and mint sprigs, for garnish	

Preheat the oven to 350°F (175°C). Peel, halve and core the pears, leaving the stem attached to one half of each pear. Place the pears flat side down in a 9- x 13-inch (23- x 33-cm) baking pan. Pour the wine over the pears. Sprinkle the saffron threads over the pears, making sure that some of the threads land on the pears. Disperse the star anise pods and the peppercorns in the pan. Drizzle the honey over the pears. Place the pan on the centre rack of the oven and bake for 1 hour, basting and turning the pears every 10 to 15 minutes. Test the pears with a toothpick. They should be soft but not mushy. Allow to cool. (The pears and juice can now be refrigerated in an airtight container for a day. Allow to return to room temperature prior to serving.)

To serve, place one half of a pear on the plate and lean the other half against the first. Drizzle the plate with the sauce, star anise and peppercorns. Garnish with the whipped cream and mint. Serve immediately.

Rosemary & Pear Cider Sorbet with Cider-Poached Pear

This is a simple two-for-one approach. Make a syrup, poach the pears in the syrup, then purée and freeze half the pears with half the syrup. Serve the sorbet with the rest of the poached pears. Allow half a pear per person as a palate cleanser, a whole pear each as a dessert.

Serves 6   DEE HOBSBAWN-SMITH

6	12-oz. (340-mL) bottles pear cider	6
	sugar to taste	
2 cups	water	480 mL
2	lemons or limes, juice and zest	2
2	oranges, juice and zest	2
4	whole star anise	4
1 tsp.	whole allspice	5 mL
6	quarter-sized slices fresh ginger	6
2	sticks cinnamon	2
3–4	sprigs fresh rosemary	3–4
1 tsp.	whole peppercorns	5 mL
8	whole cloves	8
12	near-ripe pears, peeled and cored	12
6	sprigs rosemary, for garnish	6
6	whole star anise, for garnish	6

Combine everything but the pears and garnishes in a large pot. Bring to a boil, then simmer for 10 to 20 minutes, or until the syrup has acquired flavour and spice. Strain if desired, then add the peeled whole pears. Cover with parchment paper cut to size and a lid, and gently cook on medium heat until the pears are tender. To test, pierce a pear with a fork; the fork should slide easily in and out.

Cool the pears in the liquid and store covered in the fridge. Remove the pears and set aside half. Strain the liquid and divide it in half. Purée half the pears with half the liquid. Freeze in an ice cream maker. Cook the remaining liquid until it has reduced to a thick syrup.

To serve, slice the pears in half and place on a scoop of pear sorbet. Spoon the syrup over top. Garnish with the rosemary and whole star anise.

Caramel Roasted Pears with Pernod Ice Cream

Make this in fall or early winter when pears are at their prime. The pear must be a firm type—Anjou is best—and not too ripe or it will fall apart. The Pernod ice cream is another example of my ongoing love of licorice.

Pam Fortier

Serves 4

1 cup	brown sugar	240 mL
½ cup	unsalted butter	120 mL
4	Anjou pears, slightly underripe	4
¼ cup	water	60 mL
½ cup	whipping cream	120 mL
4 scoops	Pernod Ice Cream	4 scoops

Preheat the oven to 325°F (165°C). Place the brown sugar and butter in a baking dish large enough to hold all the pears lying on their sides. Put the baking dish in the oven to melt the butter while you prepare the pears.

Leaving the stems intact, carefully peel the pears. Use a melon-baller to remove the core at the bottom, then scoop out higher inside the pears to remove the seeds and fibrous part around them.

Remove the baking dish from the oven and stir to combine the melted butter and brown sugar. Add the water and mix together. Place the pears on their sides in the dish, coating each one thoroughly with the caramel mixture. Roast for approximately 2 hours, turning and basting the pears with the caramel every 15 minutes. When done the pears should be soft when pierced with a small sharp knife. Remove the dish from the oven.

Stand each pear upright in an attractive serving dish or bowl. Carefully pour the caramel into a saucepan. Place on medium-high heat. Stir in the cream and allow the mixture to boil for a minute or two to combine. Strain if desired, or serve the sauce as is over the pears. Place a scoop of ice cream alongside each pear.

Pernod Ice Cream

Makes 1 quart (1 L)

2 cups	whole milk	480 mL
1 cup	sugar	240 mL
8	egg yolks	8
2 cups	whipping cream	480 mL
4 Tbsp.	Pernod	60 mL

Heat the milk in a medium-sized pot over medium-high heat until steaming. Place the sugar and egg yolks in a bowl and whisk to combine. Slowly pour the scalded milk over the yolks and sugar, whisking continuously. When combined, pour the mixture back into the same pot and place over medium-high heat. Stir constantly with a wooden spoon. Do not allow it to boil. The mixture will thicken slightly and coat the back of the spoon. Immediately strain it into a clean bowl. Add the whipping cream and Pernod. If you wish a stronger flavour, add another tablespoon (15 mL) of Pernod. Chill the mixture, then process in an ice cream maker.

Hazelnut & White Chocolate Blondies with Whiskey Ice Cream

Cut these butterscotch "chocolateless" brownies into triangles and serve topped with the whiskey ice cream for a delicious dessert.

Pam Fortier

MAKES 1 8-INCH (20-CM) SQUARE PAN

½ cup	unsalted butter, at room temperature	120 mL
1¼ cups	brown sugar	300 mL
½ tsp.	vanilla extract	2.5 mL
1	egg	1
1 cup	all-purpose flour	240 mL
1¼ tsp.	baking powder	6.2 mL
½ cup	coarsely chopped good-quality white chocolate	120 mL
½ cup	hazelnuts that have been toasted, skinned and coarsely chopped	120 mL
8 scoops	Whiskey Ice Cream	8 scoops

Line an 8-inch (20-cm) square pan with parchment paper. This is easier if you spray the pan with cooking spray first. Preheat the oven to 325°F (165°C).

Cream the butter in a mixer with the paddle attachment (or by hand for 2 to 3 minutes). Add the brown sugar and continue mixing. Add the vanilla extract and egg and mix to combine. Scrape down the bowl. Combine the flour and baking powder and add all at once, mixing just until combined. Mix in the chocolate and nuts by hand to avoid overmixing. Pour into the prepared pan and bake for 15 to 20 minutes. When done the centre will still appear slightly liquid if pressed, but the sides will be pulling away from the pan.

Cool before cutting into triangles. Serve each triangle topped with a scoop of ice cream.

TOASTING AND SKINNING HAZELNUTS

Place the nuts on a baking sheet and bake at 350°F (175°C) for 8 to 10 minutes, or until fragrant. Remove from the oven and place the nuts on a clean kitchen towel. Place your hands under the towel and rub them together, rubbing the nuts against each other and the towel to remove the skins.

Pam Fortier

WHISKEY ICE CREAM

MAKES 1 QUART (1 L)

3 cups	whipping cream	720 mL
1 cup	homogenized milk	240 mL
8	egg yolks	8
1 cup	sugar	240 mL
1 tsp.	vanilla extract	5 mL
4 Tbsp.	whiskey	60 mL

Place 1 cup (240 mL) of the whipping cream and the milk in a medium-sized, heavy saucepan and heat to just under a boil. Place the egg yolks in a bowl, add the sugar and whisk to combine. When the cream mixture is hot, add it slowly to the egg yolk mixture, whisking constantly. Pour back into the pot. Cook over medium-high heat, stirring constantly with a wooden spoon, until it is slightly thickened. (Do not allow it to boil or the mixture will turn into "scrambled eggs.") When it coats the back of the wooden spoon, immediately strain it into a clean bowl. Add the remaining 2 cups (480 mL) cream, vanilla extract and whiskey. Cool completely and process in an ice cream maker.

ROSEWATER & SAGE ICE CREAM

Inspired by ice cream that I had at Moro, a restaurant in London, England, this version has the indigenous prairie flavours of rose (think Alberta wild rose!) and sage. Rosewater is often used in Middle Eastern cooking and can be sourced through any specialty food store or local Middle Eastern grocery. Steeping fresh Alberta wild rose petals for a rosewater tea is an authentic way to make a local ice cream. Gum mastic (or gum arabic) is an unusual ingredient that is entirely optional. It is sometimes used in ice cream and jam to prevent crystallization and is available in Middle Eastern specialty stores.

RHONDDA SIEBENS

SERVES 8

1 Tbsp.	ground sage	15 mL
2½ cups	whole milk	600 mL
2½ cups	whipping cream	600 mL
1	cinnamon stick	1
3	crystals gum mastic, crushed (optional)	3
¾ cup	fine granulated white sugar	180 mL
1 cup	rosewater	240 mL
1	14-oz. (398-mL) can evaporated milk	1
	dried rose petals, for garnish	

Combine the sage, milk, cream and cinnamon stick in a large heavy saucepan. Heat over medium heat until bubbles appear and the mixture is about to boil. Simmer for approximately 20 minutes to reduce it somewhat. Stir in the crushed gum mastic, if using, and set aside to cool. Remove the cinnamon stick.

Meanwhile, dissolve the sugar in the rosewater in a small saucepan over low heat. Simmer to form a thin syrup, at least 15 minutes. Set aside to cool.

Add the evaporated milk to the cooled milk and cream mixture, and then combine with the rosewater syrup. Process in an ice cream maker according to manufacturer's directions.

Serve with dried rose petals on top.

Cinnamon Panna Cotta

Silky as a really fine negligee, panna cotta is a subtle invitation to other things. Don't complicate matters by lily-gilding. Just serve it, send your guests home early and let matters take their own course. Serve with a fresh fruit compote, for garnish, if you like.

SERVES 8   DEE HOBSBAWN-SMITH

2¹/₂ tsp.	gelatin	12.5 mL
2 Tbsp.	water	30 mL
3 cups	whipping cream	720 mL
²/₃ cup	sugar	160 mL
¹/₂	vanilla bean, split lengthwise	¹/₂
2	cinnamon sticks	2
1	star anise	1

Soften the gelatin in the water in a small bowl. Heat the cream, sugar, vanilla bean, cinnamon sticks and star anise in a heavy pot and let simmer until the spice flavours permeate the cream, about 15 to 20 minutes. Strain. Stir in the dissolved gelatin. Heat the cream a bit more to melt the gelatin if it isn't dissolved.

Divide the mixture among 8 ramekins and chill for at least 2 hours. To serve, unmould each dessert by running a hot knife run around the inside of the mould. Invert the panna cotta onto a plate.

La Bomba with Strawberry & Ginger Mousse

Nut tortes don't always include flour, but this one does, for a little extra stability and finer texture—important when you consider the cake is a container for mousse! Choose a nut whose flavour and smell you enjoy—hazelnuts are wonderful with dark chocolate, and so are toasted almonds. Pistachios make a wonderful green cake that provides unexpected contrast to the pink mousse and the dark glaze. Adventurous cooks have room for experimentation in this eggless mousse. Substitute raspberry, mango or peach purée for the strawberry purée. Change the white chocolate to milk chocolate and replace the fruit and ginger with chopped hazelnuts; change the chocolate to semi-sweet and add a hint of ground cinnamon for a richer, darker, more mysterious mousse. This dessert deserves to be served in plain sight of your guests. Small slices only—it is unabashedly rich!

DEE HOBSBAWN-SMITH   SERVES 16

¾ lb.	toasted nuts, skinned if necessary	340 g
½ cup	all-purpose flour	120 mL
	pinch salt	
12	eggs, separated	12
1⅓ cups	granulated sugar	320 mL
½ tsp.	vanilla extract	2.5 mL
1 recipe	Strawberry and Ginger Mousse	1 recipe
1 recipe	Chocolate and Honey Rum Glaze	1 recipe

Preheat the oven to 375°F (190°C). Line a 17½- x 13-inch (4.4- x 33-cm) baking sheet with parchment.

Combine the nuts with half the flour and the salt in a food processor and grind to a fine but not powdery consistency. Using a mixer, beat the egg yolks, half the sugar and the vanilla on high speed until they triple in volume. Set aside. In a clean bowl with a clean whisk, whisk the egg whites and the remaining sugar until the whites triple in volume and achieve stiff peaks.

Gently fold one-third of the whites into the yolk mixture, cutting and folding to equalize the different textures. Dust half the nut-flour mixture over top, and fold it and half the remaining egg whites into the mixture. Repeat with the remaining nut-flour mixture and egg white mixture, being careful to fold only enough to incorporate but not to deflate. No egg whites or dry ingredients should be visible; it should be one smooth, homogeneous batter.

Gently spread the batter over the parchment-lined tray. Bake for 23 minutes, or until just set.

Remove the cake from the oven. Invert the cake onto a cloth-lined counter. Invert a glass or stainless steel bowl 3 inches (7.5 cm) deep and $9\frac{1}{2}$ inches (24 cm) in diameter onto the cake and cut a circle from the cake. Set the circle aside. Line the bowl with plastic wrap. Use the remaining cake to tidily line the bowl, forming a solid lining of cake. Cool.

Fill the cooled cake bowl with mousse. Smooth the surface and lay the circular piece of cake over top, fitting it snugly. Wrap securely and chill overnight.

Unwrap and invert the cake onto a round plate. Remove the plastic wrap. Drizzle the softened glaze over the bombe to form a smooth coating. Chill well.

To serve, slice with a hot, thin-bladed knife. Clean the knife between each slice.

STRAWBERRY AND GINGER MOUSSE

MAKES ABOUT 4 CUPS (950 mL)

$\frac{3}{4}$ lb.	white chocolate, finely chopped	340 g
$\frac{1}{2}$ cup	boiling milk	120 mL
2 Tbsp.	honey or sugar	30 mL
3 Tbsp.	sunflower oil	45 mL
2 Tbsp.	amber rum	30 mL
2 Tbsp.	vanilla extract	30 mL
$1\frac{1}{2}$ cups	whipping cream, whipped to firm peaks	360 mL
1 cup	strawberry purée, seeded	240 mL
2 Tbsp.	finely grated fresh ginger	30 mL

Combine the chocolate, milk, honey or sugar and oil in a large bowl. Mix well. Cool, then fold in the rum, vanilla, cream, strawberry purée and ginger. Chill.

CONTINUED OVER PAGE. . .

Chocolate and Honey Rum Glaze

Makes about 1½ cups (360 mL)

6 Tbsp.	unsalted butter	90 mL
6 oz.	semi-sweet chocolate, chopped	170 g
2 Tbsp.	honey	30 mL
1 Tbsp.	amber rum	15 mL

Combine the butter, chocolate and honey in a heatproof bowl. Microwave on medium power for 2 to 3 minutes, stirring several times. Remove from the microwave and stir in the rum. Cool to glazing consistency.

Tarte au FROMAGE Blanc
(Curd CHEESE Tart)

RECOMMENDED WINE:
served as a savoury dish, it
would pair well with a light
riesling or muscat

Fromage blanc, also known as curd cheese, is a soft, fresh cream cheese with the consistency of sour cream that is popular in Europe. This tart is a perfect ending to a summer meal as it is not sweet. Try substituting mascarpone or a soft cream cheese if you can't find the real thing. A few fresh berries or a compote adds a sweet touch.

MAKES 1 11-INCH (28-CM) TART   RHONDDA SIEBENS

For the pastry:

1½ cups	all-purpose flour	360 mL
1½ tsp.	sugar	7.5 mL
½ tsp.	kosher salt	2.5 mL
¼ cup	cold water	60 mL
½ cup	unsalted butter, cold	120 mL

In a food processor fitted with a steel blade, combine the flour, sugar and salt. Add the water and as you continue to pulse, add the butter in small increments, pulsing until the dough just begins to come together. Gather into a ball, wrap in plastic, and refrigerate for at least 1 hour.

Roll the dough out on a floured work surface to ⅛ inch (.3 cm) thick. Trim and fit the pastry into your tart pan.

For the filling:

1⅛ lbs.	fromage blanc, well drained	510 g
⅓ cup	all-purpose flour	80 mL
⅓ cup	half-and-half	80 mL
2	eggs	2
½ tsp.	salt	2.5 mL
	pinch freshly ground black pepper	
¼ cup	butter	60 mL

Preheat the oven to 400°F (200°C). Mix all the ingredients together, except for the butter. Pour into the unbaked tart shell. Dot the top with pieces of butter and bake for approximately 45 minutes. Serve cold.

"CREAMSICLE" TART

I didn't set out to create a tart that tasted like a Creamsicle, I was just combining some of my favourite flavours. Blood oranges make an especially beautiful tart, but when they are not in season feel free to use regular oranges. I like the contrast of candied orange peel, which remains slightly bitter, with the sweetness of the white chocolate filling. The pastry is based on a recipe by Carol Field, from her classic, *The Italian Baker*.

PAM FORTIER   SERVES 10 TO 12

For the pastry:

½ cup	sugar	120 mL
¾ cup + 2 Tbsp.	unsalted butter	210 mL
1	egg	1
1 tsp.	vanilla extract	5 mL
2¼ cups	all-purpose flour	535 mL
	pinch salt	

Cream the sugar and butter together in a mixer with a paddle attachment for 2 to 3 minutes on medium speed. Combine the egg and vanilla extract and add to the butter and sugar. Mix for a minute or so, then scrape down the bowl and mix again. Combine the flour and salt. Add to the bowl and mix only until the dough holds together. Shape into a disk, wrap in plastic and chill for at least an hour. (If making by hand, combine the flour, sugar and salt in a bowl. Cut the butter in with a pastry blender or two knives until a coarse, meal-like texture is obtained. Combine the egg and vanilla and stir into the mixture. Squeeze together to form a disk.)

Allow the dough to soften at room temperature for approximately 15 minutes before rolling. Preheat the oven to 400°F (200°C). Divide the dough in half. Wrap one piece in plastic and freeze for later use. Shape the remaining piece into a disk again. On a floured surface, roll out to a 13-inch (33-cm) circle. Fit into an 11-inch (28-cm) tart pan with a removable bottom. Press into the corners and trim the edges. Bake for 20 to 25 minutes, or until golden brown. Cool.

CRÈME FRAÎCHE

Crème fraîche is a cultured, or "soured," and thickened cream much more readily available for purchase in Europe than North America. Its creaminess and slightly sour tang perfectly complements the sweetness of most desserts and makes it an interesting alternative to whipped cream. To make crème fraîche at home, combine 2 parts whipping cream with 1 part sour cream. Whisk well to smooth out the lumps, cover loosely and leave at room temperature overnight. Cover and refrigerate to thicken further.

PAM FORTIER

For the crème fraîche ganache:

12 oz.	good-quality white chocolate, chopped	340 g
1 cup	crème fraîche	240 mL

Combine the chocolate and crème fraîche in a glass bowl or measuring cup. Microwave on medium until melted. Heat 3 minutes at a time, stirring at each interval until melted.

Pour into the cooled tart shell. Chill for at least 3 hours.

For the oranges:

1 cup	sugar	240 mL
2 cups	water	480 mL
3	blood oranges (2 if using navel oranges)	3

Heat the sugar and water in a saucepan over medium heat to dissolve the sugar. Slice the oranges into slices approximately $\frac{1}{16}$ to $\frac{1}{8}$ inch (.3 to .6 cm) thick, using a sharp knife. Blood oranges tend to break up more, so allow 3 oranges to have enough perfect slices. Slide the slices into the sugar water. Increase the heat and bring it almost to a boil, then turn it down and simmer for 30 to 45 minutes, or until the white pith just under the zest has become almost clear. Remove the slices to a strainer, reserving the liquid. Add any drained juice to the pot. Turn the heat to high and cook to reduce the liquid to a syrupy consistency.

To finish the tart:

While the orange liquid is reducing, arrange the orange slices over the white chocolate layer in the tart pan. Start at the outside, just in from the pastry, and overlap the slices by half. Place 4 slices in the centre. When the liquid starts to look syrupy, remove from the heat. Using a pastry brush, glaze the orange slices. Serve immediately or refrigerate for up to 2 days. Cut with a sharp knife.

Almond QUESADILLAS with Sautéed
NECTARINES & MASCARPONE Cream

This is a sweet version of a savoury dish that's fun to eat. Make the crêpes, mascarpone cream and sautéed nectarines in advance, and fill the crêpes just before serving. You can also caramelize the fruit just before you fill and serve the crêpes— which makes for a nice contrast of textures and temperatures.

CINDA CHAVICH   SERVES 6 TO 8

For the crêpes:

³/₄ cup	flour	180 mL
³/₄ cup	finely ground almonds	180 mL
¹/₄ cup	sugar	60 mL
2	large eggs	2
1¹/₂ cups	milk	360 mL
1 tsp.	vanilla extract	5 mL
3 Tbsp.	melted butter	45 mL

Combine the flour, almonds, sugar, eggs, milk, vanilla extract and 1 Tbsp. (15 mL) of the melted butter in a blender and blend until smooth. Set the batter, in the blender container, in the refrigerator for 1 hour.

Heat a non-stick 8-inch (20-cm) crêpe pan over medium-high heat and brush with a little melted butter. When the pan is hot, pour in about ¹/₄ cup (60 mL) of the batter and tilt the pan so that it covers the surface. Cook until the crêpe is dry and the underside is beginning to colour, about 1 minute, then flip the crêpe and cook the second side for 30 seconds. Cool the crêpes on a rack and stack, separated by pieces of waxed paper. Cover and refrigerate.

For the mascarpone cream:

1 cup	mascarpone cheese	240 mL
1	large lemon, juice and zest	1
½ cup	whipping cream	120 mL
½ cup	icing sugar	120 mL

Beat the mascarpone, lemon juice and zest together. Beat the whipping cream with the icing sugar until stiff, then fold into the mascarpone mixture. Cover and refrigerate.

For the nectarine filling:

2 Tbsp.	butter	30 mL
2 Tbsp.	brown sugar	30 mL
5	medium nectarines, pitted and sliced into thin wedges	5

Heat the butter and brown sugar in a non-stick sauté pan over medium-high heat. Add the nectarines and cook for about 10 minutes, just until they are beginning to caramelize. Set aside.

Additional ingredients:

	sifted icing sugar	
½ cup	fresh raspberries and/or blueberries, for garnish	120 mL

To make the quesadillas, spread some of the mascarpone cream over each crêpe, top with a single layer of sautéed fruit and a second crêpe. Press lightly to seal. Cut each into 6 or 8 wedges and arrange on individual dessert plates. Garnish the plates with a dusting of icing sugar and a sprinkling of fresh berries.

Brie in Silk Pyjamas with Brioche Crostini

This looks like a million bucks on a buffet table and makes a great dessert. But do not be tempted to substitute sweet cherries for the sour ones—it will make too sweet a compote. The extra loaf of brioche can be frozen—if you can resist eating it.

DEE HOBSBAWN-SMITH

SERVES 10 TO 20 CHEESE-LOVERS

1/2 cup	dried sour cherries	120 mL
1/4–1/2 cup	water	60–120 mL
1 cup	plum jam	240 mL
2 Tbsp.	blackcurrant jam	30 mL
1 Tbsp.	minced fresh thyme	15 mL
1	lemon, juice and zest	1
12	sheets phyllo pastry	12
1/2 cup	melted butter	120 mL
1	2-lb. (1-kg) wheel ripe Brie	1
1	loaf Brioche	1

Rehydrate the cherries in the water, simmering them on the stovetop or in the microwave until tender. Let stand to absorb any water, then stir in the plum jam, blackcurrant jam, thyme, lemon juice and zest. Refrigerate this compote until needed.

Place a sheet of phyllo on your work surface and brush with butter. Place a second sheet on top at an offset angle, and lightly butter it. Repeat with 4 more sheets, turning each so that a rough circle of phyllo is the end result. Centre the Brie on the stack of phyllo. Fold the edges up and around the cheese, patting them flat.

On an adjacent space, repeat with the remaining 6 sheets of phyllo, again forming it into a rough circle. Lift the entire circle and lay it on top of the Brie, folding the edges down and tucking them under the bottom. Transfer the entire wheel to a parchment-lined baking sheet with a lip. Chill, covered.

Make crostini by thinly slicing the brioche and toasting it under a broiler.

Preheat the oven to 375°F (190°C). Bake the Brie for 15 to 25 minutes, or until the phyllo is brown. Slide it onto a decorative plate with a lip. Spoon the compote onto the plate all around the cheese. Arrange the crostini in a basket close by. Serve hot.

Phyllo Dough

Don't be intimidated by phyllo. It's easy, quicker than most other kinds of pastry, and it doesn't need a rolling pin. First, make sure you buy your phyllo in a store with a high turnover rate. If it's old, or if it's been thawed and re-frozen, phyllo can be brittle and dry.

Carefully thawed phyllo is pliable and easy to use. Choose a work area that is large enough to accommodate the entire stack once you have unrolled it, then add the same length of counter again so you have room to lay out and work with one sheet at a time. Keep the sheets you're not working with covered with plastic wrap to prevent drying and cracking. If you've gotten this far with phyllo, treat it with respect—brush it with butter, nothing less.

DEE HOBSBAWN-SMITH

Cinnamon buns: Increase the eggs to 4 and the sugar to I cup (240 mL) when making the dough. Generously butter an 18- x 13-inch (45- x 33-cm) baking sheet with sides or two 9- x 13-inch (23- x 33-cm) cake pans. Sprinkle with brown sugar. Roll the dough into a large rectangle, 26 x 14 inches (65 x 35 cm). Brush with melted butter, sprinkle with brown sugar, and sprinkle on cinnamon and raisins. Roll it up, jelly roll-style. Cut in half, using a metal pastry scraper, then in quarters. Cut each quarter into 6. Place the rolls, cut side up, on the pan. Let rise for about 20 minutes, then bake at 375°F (190°C) for 20 to 30 minutes, until just done. Invert onto a tray as soon as you remove them from the oven. Serve warm.

BRIOCHE

MAKES 2 LOAVES

2 Tbsp.	active dry yeast	30 mL
2 Tbsp.	sugar	30 mL
1/2 cup	warm-to-hot water or milk	120 mL
2	large eggs	2
4 cups	all-purpose flour	950 mL
1/2 cup	sugar	120 mL
1 Tbsp.	kosher salt	15 mL
1 cup	warm-to-hot water or milk	240 mL
1 lb.	soft unsalted butter	450 g

In a countertop mixer, combine the yeast, the 2 Tbsp. (30 mL) sugar and 1/2 cup (120 mL) water or milk. Let this mixture stand for about 5 minutes, until it is puffy. This shows that the yeast is alive and active. Add the eggs, flour, 1/2 cup (120 mL) sugar, salt and 1 cup (240 mL) water or milk. Mix with the dough hook until it is a smooth ball. Turn it out onto the counter and knead until smooth and soft, at least 5 minutes.

Smear the butter into the dough by the handful, until it is completely incorporated. Butter the bowl, turn the dough into the bowl, cover with plastic wrap and put in a warm place to rise. (We often turn the oven on very low for a few minutes, then turn it off and place the dough in to rise.)

When the dough has doubled in bulk (about 40 to 60 minutes in a warm room), punch it down. Divide it into 2 equal pieces. Knead each until smooth, about 2 minutes, and shape into two 12-inch (30-cm) loaves. Generously butter two 12- x 4- x 8-inch (30- x 7.5- x 10-cm) pans. Place the loaves in the pans and let rise again until double in bulk, about 1/2 hour.

Preheat the oven to 375°F (190°C). Bake the bread on the middle rack until nicely brown and crusty. It should sound hollow when you tap on the bottom. Cool on a rack.

My Dinner Party from Hell

I had offered to host a farewell dinner party for a very good friend who was particularly interested in food. Gathered together was a diverse group of friends and work colleagues, many of whom I didn't know very well. Predicting the success of the evening was like rolling dice.

It started out well. George parked himself at the kitchen counter to chat while we prepared dinner. Little did we know that he was also guzzling quantities of wine, so he was the first casualty. By the time we served dinner, he turned a whiter shade of pale when presented with the star anise-laced squash soup charmingly finished with a swish of crème fraîche. The alcohol in George also inspired him to over-react when, during a conversation, we were gently teasing his friend Tom. He leaped from the table shouting "You obviously don't understand how important Tom is to the world! You have no right to speak to him like that!" In a rage he stomped out of the house. We all thought he had gone outside for fresh air and to calm down, but discovered later that he had driven home (thankfully arriving safely)—without his shoes.

The next casualty was Eric. Eric left the table shortly after an exceptional roasted red pepper hazelnut pesto with grilled vegetables, lentil salad and grilled duck was served. Time passed at the table with conversation and laughter, until Jancis realized Eric had not returned. With a worried look on her face, she went to find him. He was sitting on the stairs leading to the basement breathing very carefully. Jancis whipped back into the dining room, wide-eyed and just short of hysterical. "Did the dinner have nuts in it?" I responded in equally wide-eyed terror, "YES!"

Trying to say "anaphylactic shock" to the 911 operator is a mouthful at the best of times; in a panic situation it is darned near impossible. After several attempts, it deteriorated into, "He's having a nut fit!" Both a fire truck and an ambulance arrived in an amazingly short time and Eric was whisked off to the hospital and successfully treated.

The rest of us—still shaking—assembled in the music room to discuss the events of the evening and listen to a CD featuring an unfortunately whiny female voice. Thinking I had heard an odd sound, I asked what it was and Anthony calmly replied, "The fire alarm." After a pause, I said, "Naa, it's just the whiny vocalist."

A minute or two later, Anthony again suggested the fire alarm had gone off. Not believing him, I nevertheless went into the kitchen to check and found charred bits floating in the air. I followed the black bits to their origin in the bathroom, where the candle holder was in full flame. Fortunately, it had fallen into the sink, so the threat of the fire spreading was minimal, but the black soot from this little piece of burning plastic was unbelievable. It was everywhere. We nearly had to summon the fire trucks a second time that night.

And, finally—could anything else possibly happen?—Anthony went to use the upstairs bathroom since the downstairs one was occupied by flames and soot and he unintentionally walked in on my roommate, Romana, who was having a leisurely bath.

No dinner party since has been able to even come close to that matchless night. But, hey, the food was good. And there are enough stories to tell for years. Life in the food business sometimes seems to lurch from one anecdote to another!

GAIL NORTON

Simply Entertaining

I must be frank and admit that the whole focus of entertaining my friends and family revolves around one major theme—simplicity. This does not arise because of "simple flavours" or some other culinary bent; it's a matter of being lazy at the end of the day and wanting to visit with my friends.

Think back to those dinner parties when you were stressed and spent every minute in the kitchen. I make a conscious effort now to pare down a meal so I can enjoy myself and, most importantly, spend time with the people I've invited over. I choose menu items that can be prepared ahead of time. Desserts such as home-made ice cream can be made days in advance and are always impressive. And there's a reason the summer barbecue is a perennial favourite—most likely everyone will be on the patio with you while you cook.

In this day and age, when eating out is commonplace, any home-cooked meal is appreciated more than ever, so don't exhaust yourself trying to serve a five-course meal if you're not inclined to do so. Entertaining does not necessarily mean putting together a whole meal with all the trimmings. I found myself this past summer doing most of my "entertaining" in my backyard over a bottle of wine and a quickly assembled platter of cheese, bread, olives, caperberries and tomatoes (or whatever happened to be handy). A very pure form of entertaining, to be sure—food, wine, friends—what more could someone ask for?

Rhondda Siebens

INDEX BY AUTHORS